Two Wonders

*Studies in the Death
and
Resurrection of
Jesus Christ*

Justin Imel

Copyright © 2002 by Justin Imel

Two Wonders
by Justin Imel

Printed in the United States of America

Library of Congress Control Number: 2002113254
ISBN 1-591602-25-4

All rights reserved. No part of this publication may be reproduced or transmitted in any form or by any means without written permission of the publisher.

Scriptures taken from the New King James Version. Copyright © 1982 by Thomas Nelson, Inc. Used by permission. All rights reserved.

Xulon Press
11350 Random Hills Road
Suite 800
Fairfax, VA 22030
(703) 279-6511
XulonPress.com

To order additional copies, call 1-866-909-BOOK (2665).

This work is lovingly dedicated to my wife,
Tammy LeAnn.
Without her support, this volume would not have been possible.

Who can find a virtuous wife?
For her worth is far above rubies.
The heart of her husband safely trusts her;
So he will have no lack of gain.
She does him good and not evil
All the days of her life.

Her children rise up and call her blessed;
Her husband also, and he praises her:
"Many daughters have done well,
But you excel them all."
— Proverbs 31:10–12, 28–29.

Table of Contents

Preface		ix
Chapter One:	Pictures from the Cross	11
Chapter Two:	The Suffering Servant	19
Chapter Three:	Surveying the Wondrous Cross	29
Chapter Four:	Surely This Was the Son of God	37
Chapter Five:	The Blood of the Lamb	47
Chapter Six:	The Greatest Death	55
Chapter Seven:	The Good Shepherd	63
Chapter Eight:	From the Mouth of a Dying Man	69
Chapter Nine:	Did Jesus Really Rise from the Dead?	77
Chapter Ten:	He's Alive	89
Chapter Eleven:	Jesus Finds Two Disciples	95
Chapter Twelve:	The Confession of a Doubter	103
Chapter Thirteen:	If the Dead Stay Dead	111

Preface

Many years ago, a well-known Christian writer lay on his deathbed. Among his last words, he was heard to say, "When I get to heaven, I shall see three wonders there. The first wonder will be to see many people there whom I did not expect to see; the second wonder will be to miss many people whom I did expect to see; and the third and greatest wonder of all will be to find myself there." Finding ourselves in heaven will be an enormous wonder.

Yet, there are two great wonders that occurred here on earth: the death and resurrection of Jesus. Why would Jesus leave the splendor of heaven to die for me at Calvary? Could he really love me that much? How could he endure such pain and anguish as he died? Jesus' death is a great wonder.

But, his resurrection stands as a great wonder also. How can a man who was crucified be raised from the dead? What implications does his resurrection have for me? Will I be raised just as he was? Will I be reunited with my deceased loved ones because Jesus was raised? Jesus' resurrection is a great wonder.

This work looks at these two wonders. Through the pages of this book, may you see the death and resurrection of Jesus as they are presented in Scripture. May you come to a deeper appreciation of what Jesus did for us. May you come to worship him more reverently and serve him more earnestly as a result.

Justin Imel
Alum Creek, West Virginia
June 2002

CHAPTER ONE:

Pictures from the Cross

Gail looked intently at her mother's hand. It was curled into a ball and covered with scars. Gail noticed that her mother had great difficulty using her hand. She could barely grasp a pen—this caused her writing to be nearly illegible. Finally, Gail could stand the mystery no longer; she asked her mother, "Mommy, why does your hand look like that?" Her mother replied, "Honey, when you were a month old, our house caught fire. Your dad ran and grabbed your brother, and I reached in your crib to get you. I had to reach through flames, and my hand suffered many burns. Sweetheart, my hand was deformed for you."

Before the advent of the modern automobile, horses pulling a buggy ran through the streets of a Georgian town. A gentleman ran after the horses, grabbed the reigns, and was dragged down the street, but he would not let go. Finally, after great effort, this stranger brought the horses to a stop. He lay in the road, bleeding and dying. Before he died, the townspeople asked this stranger why he would die to bring those horses to a stop. In great agony, the man said, "Look in the buggy," and then died. Safe and sound in the buggy was the man's infant child. He died to rescue his son.

Any parent worth anything would happily give his life for his child. How many parents have laid down their lives for their children? An intruder enters the house, and the father uses his body as a shield to prevent a bullet from ripping through his child's body. A child runs into a busy street, and a mother runs after her child, forgetting her own safety to rescue her baby.

Although parents readily give their lives for their own children, how many would readily give their lives for their enemies? How many would die for one who abused them, swore at them, spit at them, or defrauded them? Yet, that's exactly what Jesus did for us. "God demonstrates His own love toward us, in that while we were still sinners, Christ died for us" (Romans 5:8).

In this chapter, we consider the suffering Jesus did for man.

Psalm 22 graphically portrays Jesus' sufferings while he died on the cross. One can be certain an Old Testament passage fits Jesus' life when the New Testament says it fits. We know this psalm fits Jesus' crucifixion, for Jesus quoted the opening line of this psalm while on the cross. Many scholars surmise that he may have meditated upon this psalm or quoted it in its entirety from the cross. They believe this, for we have the opening cry of this psalm on Jesus' lips. Too, before Jesus died on the cross, he cried out, "It is finished." The last line of the psalm can be translated something like "He has finished it."

Charles Spurgeon, the well-known Baptist preacher from the late 1800's, said the following of this psalm: "We should read reverently, putting off our shoes from off our feet, as Moses did at the burning bush, for if there be holy ground anywhere in Scripture it is in this psalm." In this chapter, let us take the shoes from off our feet, as it were, and see the pictures of Jesus presented in this psalm.

David presents Jesus as a forsaken Lord:

Forsaken Lord

My God, My God, why have You forsaken Me?
Why are You so far from helping Me,
And from the words of My groaning?
O My God, I cry in the daytime, but You do not hear;
And in the night season, and am not silent.
(Psalm 22:1–2)

Even in intense suffering, Jesus kept his faith in God. He cried from the cross, not merely, "God, God, why have you forsaken me?"

Rather, he cried, *"**My** God, **My** God, why have you forsaken me?"* (emphasis mine). What a profound lesson for us today—even when God seems far off, even when it seems that God does not hear, we can put our confidence in him, and know that he is our God.

Jesus attempted to understand why God had forsaken him. He knew full well why Judas and Peter had forsaken him: Judas had money in his eyes and Peter had timidity in his heart. But, how could God, his Father, the one in whom he trusted, leave him in such a perilous hour? Could one really have more agony than being forsaken by God? Not only had his friends deserted him, but God, the one who was to be there no matter what, had also deserted him.

Jesus wondered aloud why God was so far from the words of his groaning. "Groaning" literally refers to the roaring of a wild animal; the wild animal makes this sound when in great distress. Here's the idea in this context—Jesus cried so much, suffered so much, and prayed so much that he no longer had words left to express his grief. All Jesus could do after suffering for days was moan.

Jesus cried in the daytime and in the night, but God did not hear. He believed God did not hear his cries, for God did not answer the way he desired. Even though Jesus did not receive the answer he wanted, he still prayed. But Jesus knew he should still pray, for he taught his disciples to pray always. "He spoke a parable to them, that men always ought to pray and not lose heart" (Luke 18:1). Jesus remained fervent in prayer, appealing to God, for he had nowhere else to go.

A great theological mystery occurs in this text. Just how could God have separated himself from his Son? The Father and Son are one. Jesus himself said, "I and My Father are one" (John 10:30). If they are one, how could this separation take place? I, for one, do not understand.

Although it boggles the mind to consider how the Father and Son were separated while Jesus died, the reason the Father forsook the Son is not at all perplexing. God forsook Jesus as Jesus "bore our sins in His own body on the tree" (1 Peter 2:24). Because Jesus took our sins upon himself, he stood alienated from God. Those in sin are alienated from God. "You have hidden Your face from us, And have consumed us because of our iniquities" (Isaiah

64:7). "Because of the evil of their deeds I will drive them from My house; I will love them no more" (Hosea 9:15). Because of our sins, Jesus had to endure the separation from the Father that should have been ours in eternity.

God could not hear the prayers of Jesus because of our sins. God cannot answer the prayers of those in rebellion to him. "If I regard iniquity in my heart, The Lord will not hear" (Psalm 66:18). "Then they will cry to the Lord, But He will not hear them; He will even hide His face from them at that time, Because they have been evil in their deeds" (Micah 3:4). While on the cross, Jesus had iniquity in his heart, and he had evil deeds. But understand that he had our iniquity and our evil deeds in his heart.

Our sins caused Jesus to cry out, "My God, My God, why have you forsaken me?" Our sinfulness caused Jesus to endure hell in all its agony and fierceness while he hung on the cross—the times we've lost our temper with our spouses, have watched television programs to incite our lust, or have stayed home instead of worshiping with the saints. These sins and every other sin imaginable put Jesus on the cross. These sins forced the Father to abandon the Son.

Ridiculed Savior

But I am a worm, and no man;
A reproach of men, and despised by the people.
All those who see Me ridicule Me;
They shoot out the lip, they shake the head, saying,
"He trusted in the Lord, let Him rescue Him;
Let Him deliver Him, since He delights in Him!"
(Psalm 22:6–8)

Jesus was a worm, and not a man; he was a reproach of men, and despised by the people. Jesus was comparable to a worm. Worms are helpless, and when they are stepped on and killed for our own recreation, no one cares. When was the last time you lost sleep because you went fishing and pierced a worm with a hook and put it in the water for a fish to eat? Jesus was just like that worm—killed and no one cared. Jesus was reproached and despised by the people. Just how much he was despised was evident when the crowd asked for a murderer, rather than Jesus, to be handed over to them.

All the people ridiculed Jesus. Notice the text says, *"**All** those who see me ridicule Me"* (emphasis mine). The crowd ridiculed Jesus, the chief priests and scribes ridiculed him, and even the thieves ridiculed him. The people were thinking, "If this really is the Messiah, he can't be dying on a cross. He's supposed to save Israel from the Romans."

Those who saw him shot out the lip. In the East, the protruding of the lower lip was a sign of great contempt. In "shooting out the lip" to Jesus, they were saying that they considered him to be worthless, unworthy of any appreciation. Those who crucified Jesus showed contempt for Jesus during his ministry, and now, even at his death, they show him the greatest of contempt.

They said, "He trusted in the Lord, let Him rescue Him; Let Him deliver Him, since He delights in Him!" Here the ridicule the Savior endured centered on his faith in God. One's faith is immensely personal, something one holds very dear. Yet, those at the cross ridiculed Jesus for his most personal aspect: his faith.

Jesus had to endure this ridicule because of our sins. Because of sin, Jesus was forced to hang on the cross and endure this ridicule, endure this mockery. Granted, he could have walked away. Yet, had Jesus walked away, man would not have the forgiveness of his sins.

Writhing Savior

I am poured out like water,
And all My bones are out of joint;
My heart is like wax;
It is melted within Me.
My strength is dried up like a potsherd,
And My tongue clings to My jaws;
You have brought Me to the dust of death.

For dogs have surrounded Me;
The congregation of the wicked has enclosed Me.
They pierced My hands and My feet;
I can count all My bones.
They look and stare at Me.

> They divide My garments among them.
> And for My clothing they cast lots.
> (Psalm 22:14–18)

The suffering Savior was *poured out like water.* Although the exact meaning cannot be ascertained, it is probably close to extreme weakness and exhaustion. He had suffered so much in the last few hours that his body had been drained of all strength. The body can take only so much, and Jesus' body had tolerated as much as it could. His body was out of strength; his death was imminent.

Because his death was imminent, *all of his bones were out of joint.* The posture he had to assume on the cross—the posture that would produce death—caused his bones to be pulled out of joint. His hands and feet were nailed to the cross before he was hoisted into the air. As Jesus' cross went into place with a thud, his bones were pulled out of their sockets and out of joint.

His heart was like wax, melted within him. Again, extreme exhaustion is probably in view. He was so weak because his heart was melted like wax in the sun.

Jesus' strength was dried up like a potsherd. The sun beat down on the Lord's bare body, zapping him of all his strength. His strength had become like a potsherd, a broken, dry piece of pottery. He had no strength; his energy was gone.

His tongue clove to his jaws. One side effect of crucifixion was extreme thirst. When a man loses as much blood as Jesus surely did, he becomes dehydrated. The body craves liquid to replace the liquid lost through the open wounds. Our Lord suffered this intense thirst. In fact, the Lord said from the cross, "I thirst" (John 19:28).

Jesus had been *brought to the dust of death.* "Dust of death" often stands for death itself in Hebrew thought; notice verse 29: "All those who go down to the dust Shall bow before Him." Jesus was at the point of death. He had endured the torture of the cross. Now, his life ebbed away.

Jesus' hands and feet had been pierced. When one was crucified, huge spikes were driven through the wrists—which in the Orient were considered part of the hand—and the feet. The piercing of the hands and feet severed nerves in the arms and legs. This severing of nerves caused unbearable pain to shoot through one's body.

Jesus could count all his bones. Because the nerves in his arms and legs had been severed, Jesus could feel every ache in his body all the more intensely. Jesus suffered intense pain. We do anything in our power to relieve pain—we take pain medication, we refuse to go to the dentist because pain might be involved. But, while Jesus hung on the cross, he could not escape physical pain. He suffered this pain to release us of our sin.

Jesus suffered this much for our sins. Every ache, every pain the Lord endured resulted from our sins. When he instituted the Lord's Supper, Jesus said of the cup, "This is My blood of the new covenant, which is shed for many for the remission of sins" (Matthew 26:28). Peter simply states: "Christ also suffered for us" (1 Peter 2:21). He suffered greatly, but he suffered greatly for you and me.

We need to firmly fix these pictures from the cross in our minds. If we fix these images in our consciousness, how can we help but be better people? How can we live in sin when we understand what Jesus went through on account of our sins? How can we not serve Christ when we realize how greatly he has served us? How can we not give ourselves to Jesus when he gave himself for us? Have you understood what Jesus did for you? Do you live differently because of what he did?

Thought Questions

1. Why do parents give themselves so fully and so willingly to their children?

2. What would cause Charles Spurgeon to say, in reference to Psalm 22: "We should read reverently, putting off our shoes from off our feet, as Moses did at the burning bush, for if there be holy ground anywhere in Scripture it is in this psalm"?

3. How could Jesus keep personal faith in God when he felt so abandoned by God?

4. Why did God not answer Jesus' cries for help?

5. In what way was Jesus a worm?

6. Why do you think people despised Jesus so much?

7. Can you begin to imagine the pain Jesus must have suffered?

CHAPTER TWO:

The Suffering Servant

Sin brings heartache to every home. How many wives have wet their pillows over their husbands' careless words? How much sleep has eluded parents because their daughters became pregnant while still in high school? How often do we see siblings who no longer speak because a brother's greed consumes him after a parent's death? How many employers have fired their most effective employees because alcohol problems began encroaching on that effectiveness?

Just as sin brings heartache to man, sin tears God's heart asunder. Man's sins alienate him from God (see Joshua 7:11–12; Psalm 66:18; Isaiah 59:2) and cause man to be lost (Ezekiel 33:8; Romans 6:23). Because of God's love for man, he desires man to be saved; God is "not willing that any should perish but that all should come to repentance" (2 Peter 3:9). Thus, he sent Jesus into the world to suffer for man.

In light of God's great power, we would expect God to use that power to save man. He used great force to rescue the Israelites from Egyptian captivity: ten plagues descended upon Egypt, the Red Sea opened, and the Hebrews walked to safety. One would envision God coming to earth to annihilate Satan with a show of strength, so that man's salvation would be secure. But, God uses the sacrifice of his Servant, not his great power, to save man.

Scholars have long debated the identity of the Servant in Isaiah 53. Some identify him as Isaiah; others associate him with the nation of Israel. Nevertheless, this passage alludes to Jesus. Using this text, Philip preached Jesus to the eunuch. The preaching from this text produced faith in the eunuch and he obeyed Jesus in baptism (Acts 8:26–40). Jesus understood that his identity was enveloped in this text (Mark 10:33–34)—he told the disciples he was going to suffer.

In this chapter, we examine the Suffering Servant. As we study the Servant, may we better understand the suffering he did for our sins, and may we be better people for it!

The Sublimation of the Savior

"Behold, My Servant shall deal prudently; He shall be exalted and extolled and be very high" (Isaiah 52:13). The Suffering Servant would be high and lifted up. Of all the Old Testament authors, only Isaiah uses the phrase "high and lifted up;" each occurrence refers to God. Jesus, because of his deity, would be highly exalted. In reality, Jesus was "high and lifted up." The angels sang praise to God at news of his birth. The multitudes revered him. He received worship from the disciples.

Because he died for sin, Jesus would be highly exalted. Paul wrote, "Therefore God also has highly exalted Him and given Him the name which is above every name, that at the name of Jesus every knee should bow, of those in heaven, and of those on earth, and of those under the earth, and that every tongue should confess that Jesus Christ is Lord, to the glory of God the Father" (Philippians 2:9–11). Since Jesus did what no one else could do, he deserves our honor and our praise.

The Shock of the Savior

> Just as many were astonished at you,
> So His visage was marred more than any man,
> And His form more than the sons of men;
> So shall He sprinkle many nations,
> Kings shall shut their mouths at Him;

> For what had not been told them they shall see,
> And what they had not heard they shall consider.
> (Isaiah 52:14–15)

The Servant's appearance shocked those who saw him, for his image was marred beyond human form. Many use this to teach that Jesus must have been ugly even though the text does not speak of his physical appearance. Isaiah speaks of Jesus' sufferings. His sufferings severely disfigured him in a metaphorical way. Injury often disfigures one; those who have been in automobile accidents often have permanent disfigurement in one way or another. Likewise, Jesus' sufferings disfigured him.

Because of his features, Jesus' exaltation shocked the people. The kings shut their mouths at his glorification. Exaltation generally does not come to those who are so disfigured, but it did in Jesus' case. The people were shocked, the kings could say nothing, and they weren't quite sure what they should do.

Jesus baffled the people of his day; they simply had no clue what to do with him. When Jesus claimed to be bread from heaven, crowds left him. The rich young ruler sorrowfully walked away from Jesus. Pilate washed his hands of Jesus. The crowds, the rich young ruler, and Pilate were perplexed as to what they should do with Jesus. They were perplexed, for the Jews of their time expected the Messiah to come, kick the Romans out of Palestine, and establish a kingdom. However, he did nothing of the sort. Jesus came and died for man; humanity did not know what to do.

Do you know what to do with Jesus? You must do something with him. You either believe the claims he made or you don't. You either obey him because of those claims or you don't. Just what will you do?

The Spectacle of the Savior

> Who has believed our report?
> And to whom has the arm of the Lord been revealed?
> For He shall grow up before Him as a tender plant,
> And as a root out of dry ground.
> He has no form or comeliness;

> And when we see Him,
> There is no beauty that we should desire Him.
> He is despised and rejected by men,
> A Man of sorrows and acquainted with grief.
> And we hid, as it were, our faces from Him;
> He was despised, and we did not esteem Him.
> (Isaiah 53:1–3)

No one believed the report of the Israelites. Isaiah wrote this to those Jews who would, a few hundred years from his time, be in Babylonian captivity. The exiles would speak about the Messiah to their captors, but they would not be believed. In today's world, many do not believe the preaching about Jesus—they do not accept his claims, and they do not believe in his resurrection. Just like the Hebrews of old, we can wonder, "Who has believed our report?"

He would grow like a dry shoot. The dry shoot grows unwanted from the root of the tree. The shoot does nothing to benefit the tree or the gardener, so no one covets the sprout. Since the offshoot benefits no one, the limb is quickly removed and thrown away. No one wanted Jesus; he was "despised and rejected by men." Magnetic people—those who attract a large following—generally deliver the captive. But the Jews did not want this Deliverer.

Jesus, as the Deliverer, was so unwanted that the people despised him. When someone despises something, he considers that thing unworthy of attention. Many in Jesus' day refused to give him attention. Had they done so, they would have had to change their lives and leave their sin. Had they given Jesus attention, they would have followed him instead of the traditions of the elders.

Some gave Jesus some attention, but they rejected him. Those who rejected him declined to accept him as the Messiah, God's very Son. Many today have also rejected him. They refuse to accept his sovereignty over their lives. They refuse to accept his plan for their redemption. They refuse to accept his headship over the church.

Jesus suffered greatly. He endured mockery at the hands of the soldiers. He felt his flesh rip apart as the soldiers flogged him. He felt spikes sever nerves in his arms and legs. He struggled to breathe as he suffocated on the cross. No wonder Isaiah wrote that Jesus was acquainted with suffering.

Because the Servant suffered, the people hid their faces from him. All of his suffering caused the Servant's appearance to be disfigured. People have a hard time witnessing someone as grotesque in his appearance as the Servant. Although the Servant's disfigurement is metaphorical, the idea is that his suffering was horrible, beyond anything imaginable.

The Substitution of the Savior
Surely He has borne our griefs
And carried our sorrows;
Yet we esteemed Him stricken,
Smitten by God, and afflicted.
But He was wounded for our transgressions,
He was bruised for our iniquities;
The chastisement for our peace was upon Him,
And by His stripes we are healed.
All we like sheep have gone astray;
We have turned, every one, to his own way;
And the Lord has laid on Him the iniquity of us all.
(Isaiah 53:4–6)

During World War II, a German submarine caught an American transport ship in its crosshairs and launched a torpedo. The captain of the ship, seeing the torpedo heading directly for his ship, told his men, "Boys, this is it."

About that same time, a small escorting destroyer saw the same torpedo. The captain of that destroyer ordered, "Full speed ahead." The torpedo hit the destroyer, killing every sailor aboard. The captain of the warship declared, "The skipper of that ship was my best friend."

The skipper of the small destroyer sacrificed himself for his friend. Jesus sacrificed himself for us. We should have been beaten. We should have been on the cross. We should have died. But, he was willing to do it for us.

The people who saw the Messiah believed God had smitten him. Those in the Ancient Near East believed people suffered for their sins. If tragedy overtook an individual, they assumed he had sinned, thereby deserving the torment. When Job's three friends came to comfort him, they told Job to repent of his sin and ease his suffering. Bildad the Shuhite, for example, told Job, "If you would earnestly seek God and make your supplication to the Almighty, If you were pure and upright, Surely now He would awake for you, And prosper your rightful dwelling place" (Job 8:5–6). In other words, Bildad is saying: "Job, if you would simply repent of your wrongdoing, God would ease your suffering." Bildad and his cohorts bought into the myth that a man suffers for his sin.

However, our sins wounded Jesus, not his own. Indeed, he suffered on account of sin, but he suffered for our sin. The punishment that provides us peace rested upon him. "Peace" here refers to a right relationship with God. Because Jesus died for us, we can have a proper relationship with God.

This demonstrates how seriously God considers sin. Sin is so grievous that Jesus had to die to take sins away. No other way existed. The night before his crucifixion, Jesus begged the Father to find some other way, but no other way could be found.

"The House of a Thousand Terrors" once stood in Rotterdam, Holland. During the sixteenth century, Spain's King Philip II suppressed a Dutch rebellion. After they conquered Rotterdam, the Spanish soldiers went from house to house, slaughtering those they found. One family hid in the corner house and heard the soldiers approaching. A young man quickly grabbed a goat that had wandered into the house, butchered it, and swept the blood under the door.

When the soldiers reached the house, they reached to open the door, but when they eyed the blood, they concluded that other soldiers had already executed the inhabitants. One soldier said, "Let's keep going. There is blood coming from under the door; our work here is over." Likewise, Jesus' blood removes the coming terror of paying the punishment for our sins.

All we like sheep have gone astray. There is great emphasis in this verse that everyone has gone astray. Everyone has sinned. "There is no one who does not sin" (1 Kings 8:46). "There is none righteous, no, not one" (Romans 3:10). "All have sinned and fall short of the glory of God" (Romans 3:23).

One morning, four preachers met for breakfast. One said to the other three, "Since we are good friends, why don't we discuss some of our problems?" All four agreed to do so.

One spoke up and said, "Well, I have a drinking problem. I just cannot pry myself away from the bottle." Then another admitted, "I have a gambling problem. It's so bad that my family doesn't have enough money to pay the bills." The third preacher confessed, "I have a huge problem, because I'm falling in love with a married woman."

The fourth preacher remained silent. The other three insisted that he tell them what he struggled with, but he held back. "I just don't know how to tell you my problem," he said. "Don't worry," the others replied, "your secret is safe with us."

"Well, you see," he declared, "I am a horrible gossip."

Regardless of who we are, we struggle with sin. Regardless of how mature we are in Christ, we struggle with sin. All of us, like sheep, have gone astray. Therefore, we need a Savior who sacrificed himself for us.

The Submissiveness of the Savior

> He was oppressed and He was afflicted,
> Yet He opened not His mouth;
> He was led as a lamb to the slaughter,
> And as a sheep before its shearers is silent,
> So He opened not His mouth.
> (Isaiah 53:7)

At his trial, Jesus remained silent. Although he was oppressed and afflicted, Jesus did not open his mouth. Although he was led away to be executed, he did not open his mouth. One would expect a condemned man to protest his sentence. Most convicts appeal; most would vehemently fight their executions. Yet, when Jesus was facing the cross, he remained silent.

His remaining silent illustrates Jesus' willingness to die. Jesus could have opened his mouth, or he could have performed some great miracle, and he would have avoided the cross. But, he willingly died for our sins. Jesus could have asked for more than twelve legions of angels (Matthew 26:53). Jesus laid down his life of his own accord; no one took it from him (John 10:18).

No one forced Jesus to die for man's sins. He chose to do so, because of his great love for man. We readily acknowledge the Father's love. Nearly every child in Sunday school can quote John 3:16. However, let us not overlook the fact that the Son loves man as well. He would not have otherwise came to this world and died.

The Scorn of the Savior

He was taken from prison and from judgment,
And who will declare His generation?
For He was cut off from the land of the living;
For the transgressions of My people He was stricken.
And they made His grave with the wicked—
But with the rich at His death,
Because He had done no violence,
Nor was any deceit in His mouth.
(Isaiah 53:8–9)

In these sentences, Isaiah describes the unjustness of Jesus' trial. He was taken from prison and from judgment; in other words, no fairness could be found in the trail from start to finish. No one would declare his generation; this means that no one cared that Jesus left no heir. In the culture of Jesus' day, dying childless meant that one had lived a futile life.

His grave was made with the wicked. It was forbidden for Jesus to be buried among people like himself. He was far from wicked, but he died as a condemned man with condemned men. Just as his grave was with the wicked, he was with the rich in his death—he was buried in a rich man's tomb.

Although justice was taken from him, Jesus had done nothing wrong. Jesus had done no violence, and no deceit could be found in his mouth. Jesus lived a perfect life (1 Peter 2:21), yet he died for our sins. In fact, Jesus had to live a perfect life to die for sin. God always required a sacrifice without blemish. When the Passover was instituted, the lamb whose blood was placed upon the doorpost was to be "without blemish" (Exodus 12:5). Malachi condemned the Israelites for offering what was blind, lame, and sick (Malachi 1:8). Jesus serves as our sacrifice without blemish; we were redeemed "with the precious blood of Christ, as of a lamb without blemish and without spot" (1 Peter 1:19).

The Set Purpose of the Savior

Yet it pleased the Lord to bruise Him;
He has put Him to grief.
When You make His soul an offering for sin,
He shall see His seed, He shall prolong His days,
And the pleasure of the Lord shall prosper in His hand.
(Isaiah 53:10)

God put Jesus to death; it pleased the Lord to bruise him. Jesus' crucifixion did not occur by accident, for God had planned his death. Jesus was delivered into sinful hands "by the determined purpose and foreknowledge of God" (Acts 2:23). He was slain before the foundation of the world (Revelation 13:8).

Many have been sacrificed by accident. The following legend has often been told. One summer afternoon, a drawbridge operator took his four-year-old son, Sammy, to work with him. All the gears and controls fascinated Sammy. Every time a boat came down the river, Sammy's eyes gleamed as he watched his father pull the levers to lift the bridge, allowing the boat safe passage. After a while, Sammy's father missed his small child, but knowing his child had to be right around the control house, the father did not worry. A short while later, a train could be heard in the distance as it headed straight for the bridge. Sammy's father looked up to see his son playing on the huge gears that controlled the bridge. Panicked gripped him; he knew he didn't have the time to rescue Sammy and save the passengers on the train. Sammy's father closed his eyes, pulled the lever, causing the huge gears to move, which in turn caused the bridge to be in position for the train. After the train crossed the bridge, the father found Sammy's mangled body in the bridge's large gears.

That was an accident. Sammy's father never intended to sacrifice his son to save others. The cross, on the other hand, did not occur by accident. God knew what he was doing. God always intended to give his Son to save others. Mankind could not be saved without the shedding of blood (Hebrews 9:22). Man needed a perfect sacrifice to redeem him from sin. Jesus serves as that sacrifice.

We have a wonderful Savior who has saved us completely from sin. What about your sin? Has Jesus removed your sin?

Thought Questions

8. Why would one expect God to use his great power to save man?

9. Why is Jesus "high and lift up"?

10. Why did Jesus' appearance shock the people?

11. How would Jesus grow up as a dry shoot?

12. How did Jesus suffer for sin?

13. Why did Jesus remain silent at his trial?

14. In what ways was Jesus scorned?

15. How do we know the cross was no accident?

CHAPTER THREE:

Surveying the Wondrous Cross

Each Sunday, Christians remember Jesus' crucifixion. Before the Lord's Supper, we sing hymns such as "Jesus, Keep Me Near the Cross" or "When My Love to Christ Grows Weak" to paint in our consciousness the scenes of Golgotha. Men stand around the table where the Lord's Supper is prepared, and one of those men generally reads a text discussing the Lord's suffering. Before the bread and the fruit of the vine are distributed to the congregation, a brother offers prayers thanking God for his Son's sacrifice. As the congregation takes the emblems representing the Lord's body and blood, their minds see the Savior on the cross writhing in pain for their sin.

As vital as this weekly feast is to remembering the Lord's death, we dare not relegate meditating on the cross to those few minutes once every seven days. We need to contemplate the cross now and then, for Jesus' cross stands as Christianity's greatest symbol. While Jesus hung on the cross, he bore our sins in his body (1 Peter 2:24). Jesus shed his blood on the cross for the forgiveness of our sins (Matthew 26:28). "Christ also suffered once for sins" (1 Peter 3:18).

In this chapter, we examine Luke's account of Jesus' crucifixion. By studying this text, we will appraise the cross on which Jesus died. His cross is a:

Cross of Shame

There were also two others, criminals, led with Him to be put to death. And when they had come to the place called Calvary, there they crucified Him, and the criminals, one on the right hand and the other on the left. Then Jesus said, "Father, forgive them, for they do not know what they do." And they divided His garments and cast lots. And the people stood looking on. But even the rulers with them sneered, saying, "He saved others; let Him save Himself if He is the Christ, the chosen of God." The soldiers also mocked Him, coming and offering Him sour wine, and saying, "If you are the King of the Jews, save Yourself." (Luke 23:32–37)

We often envision the cross as a glorious event. We top our church steeples with crosses. We hang crosses in our homes. We put crosses on necklaces and hang them around our necks. We place them on our wedding bands. We set them on our lapels. Yet, to first-century Jews, the cross was far from glorious; it represented the worst in humanity. If a man went to the cross, he died a shameful death.

Jesus died between two thieves. Isaiah foresaw Jesus' being killed between two thieves: "He was numbered with the transgressors" (Isaiah 53:12). The authorities led Jesus through the streets of Jerusalem with two criminals, as though he himself were a rogue, a thief, or a criminal. When the procession arrived at Golgotha, the soldiers nailed Jesus to his cross between the two thieves.

Crucifixion was the Roman form of capital punishment; the cross was to the Romans what the electric chair and gas chamber are to us. Jesus' death between two thieves reminds us that crucifixion was indeed execution by the state. The two thieves with whom Jesus died were being killed for their crimes; they were paying their debts to society. That Friday when Jesus died was, more than likely, a day set aside for execution. The sinless Son of God died by capital punishment as though he were a convict.

Because crucifixion was capital punishment, the cross stood as the ultimate symbol of shame to the Romans. Cicero, the renowned Roman orator said, "Let the very name of the cross be far away from Roman citizens, not from their bodies only, but from their thoughts, their eyes, and their ears." One could not die a more humiliating death than crucifixion. However, Jesus died that humiliating death. He died as though he were a lawbreaker.

Jesus asked his Father to forgive those who crucified him. Imagine the love Jesus showed. Here he was hanging between heaven and earth in dreadful agony, but he still had the mind to pray for those who killed him. He prayed for those who wrongly testified against him. He prayed for those who wrongly condemned him to death. He prayed for those who spat in his face. He prayed for those who beat him. He prayed for those who mocked him. He prayed for those who nailed him to the cross.

What a lesson in grace that even those who physically put Jesus on the cross could receive pardon from God. On Pentecost, those whom Peter condemned of killing the Messiah cried out in horror, "Men and brethren, what shall we do?" Peter told them to repent and be baptized for the remission of their sins (Acts 2:36–38). He did not say, "Wait a minute! You killed Jesus; there isn't any hope for you. You cannot be saved." Instead, he offered them pardon if they turned to Jesus and obeyed him.

What a glorious thought! If those who condemned the Son of God to die could have their sins forgiven, surely we can. Although we may have committed horrible, unspeakable sins, we have done nothing akin to calling for Jesus' crucifixion. Regardless of what we may have done, if we turn to Jesus, we can receive God's pardon.

The soldiers divided Jesus' clothing by casting lots. Criminals were crucified without clothing; no evidence exists that cloths were even placed over the loins. Once the soldiers removed a criminal's clothing, they would divide the garments amongst themselves. The soldiers who crucified Jesus took what they wanted of his clothing, but not his coat. This coat was valuable, for it was seamless. The soldiers cast lots to determine who would take the coat (John 19:23–24). Our Lord was stripped of his clothing, which was divided among his executioners.

The leaders made fun of Jesus. The rulers said that if Jesus really were the Christ, he'd save himself; he'd come down from the cross, they said. The soldiers joined in mocking Jesus. The guards offered him sour wine, and they, too, told Jesus to save himself if he really were the Christ.

Imagine all the shame Jesus endured while he hung on the cross. So many taunted him, making fun of him and calling him names. He hung without his clothes, without any privacy, displayed before so many. He died a death reserved for outlaws, a death so horrible that Cicero exhorted Romans not to even think about the cross. Yet, through it all, he prayed for the forgiveness of those killing him.

Rembrandt painted a famous portrayal of the crucifixion. In examining the scene, an observer first notices Jesus' profound suffering. Then, he observes the reactions of those witnessing the death. Finally, the spectator catches a shadowy figure in the corner. That shadowy figure illustrates Rembrandt himself, for he realized that his sin crucified Jesus. Just as Rembrandt realized that his sins nailed Jesus to the cross, we realize that Jesus suffered all his humiliation because of our sins.

Cross of Salvation

Then one of the criminals who were hanged blasphemed Him, saying, "If You are the Christ, save Yourself and us." But the other, answering, rebuked him, saying, "Do you not even fear God, seeing you are under the same condemnation? And we indeed justly, for we receive the due reward of our deeds; but this Man has done nothing wrong." Then he said to Jesus, "Lord, remember me when You come into Your kingdom." And Jesus said to him, "Assuredly, I say to you, today you will be with Me in Paradise." (Luke 23:39–43)

One of the criminals taunted Jesus, saying, "Look, if you really are the Christ, save yourself and us." This criminal wanted to be saved from death; he had nothing like eternal salvation in view. This criminal feared death, and he wanted Jesus to climb down from the cross, destroy the soldiers guarding them, and rescue this criminal and his cohort from certain death.

How horrible it would be to die as a condemned man without any hope. Charles IX, who ordered the St. Bartholomew's Day Massacre, said shortly before he died, "What blood! What murders! I know not where I am. How will all this end? What shall I do? I am lost forever. I know it." Likewise, this criminal knew he was lost forever. He wanted Jesus to stop his death.

The other criminal reprimanded him. He said the other criminal should fear God, since nothing could keep them from death. This criminal said that he and the other bandit were dying for their offenses, but that Jesus did not deserve to die. What this criminal knew about Jesus is not altogether clear, but he knew that Jesus was dying innocently and that he had promised a kingdom.

Jesus was dying innocently. The chief priests, the elders, and all the council knew Jesus had done nothing deserving of death, for they sought false testimony against him (Matthew 26:59). Pilate knew Jesus did not deserve death. When the crowd kept chanting to crucify Jesus, Pilate asked them, "Why, what evil has He done?" (Matthew 27:23). When he could not persuade the crowd to save Jesus' life, he washed his hands and said, "I am innocent of the blood of this just Person" (Matthew 27:24).

After rebuking the other malefactor, the second thief asked Jesus to remember him when he came into his kingdom. Exactly what this criminal knew about Jesus' kingdom is not recorded, but he knew Jesus was going to establish a kingdom in the future. This convict wanted Jesus to take him into that kingdom.

After he heard this felon asking for a place in his kingdom, Jesus answered that request. He promised the thief that that very day they would be together in Paradise. The promise did not apply to some distant time; the promise would be (and was) fulfilled that very day. The idea is that once his life was over, this criminal would enjoy glory and bliss with Jesus. Jesus promised this criminal salvation; he found salvation at the cross.

Just like this criminal, we, too, find salvation at the cross. The good shepherd gave his life for his sheep (John 10:11). "When we were still without strength, in due time Christ died for the ungodly" (Romans 5:6). Christ died for our sins (1 Corinthians 15:3). He freed us from our sins through his blood (Revelation 1:5).

Cross of Surprise

> Now it was about the sixth hour, and there was darkness over all the earth until the ninth hour. Then the sun was darkened, and the veil of the temple was torn in two. And when Jesus had cried out with a loud voice, He said, "Father, 'into Your hands I commit My spirit.'" Having said this, He breathed His last. So when the centurion saw what had happened, he glorified God, saying, "Certainly this was a righteous Man!" (Luke 23:44–47)

The death of Jesus differed from the deaths of all others. When someone dies, everything goes on as before. Although the family hurts, few others even take notice. After a few days, the family goes back to work, attempts to pick up the pieces, and goes on with life, however difficult that is.

But not so when Jesus died. The natural phenomena at Jesus' death differed greatly than the natural phenomena when others die. Darkness covered the entire earth. When was the last time you remembered darkness shrouding the earth when someone passed away? The day my maternal grandfather died was a beautiful day. The October sun shined beautifully, and a mild wind cooled an abnormally warm autumn day. The sun never stopped shining. Nothing extraordinary occurred.

The veil in the temple split in two. This veil separated the Holy Place from the Holy of Holies. Only the high priest could enter the Holy of Holies, and he could go in that place only once a year on the Day of Atonement. On that holy day, the priest went into God's presence to make atonement for Israel's sins. The tearing of the curtain shows that man does not need a priest to enter God's presence. After all, all Christians are priests (1 Peter 2:9).

When Jesus died, he committed his spirit to the Father's hands. When most people die, they die in fear. They hope to be in Paradise with God, but they doubt they will actually dwell there. Jesus had no doubts. He knew he would receive glory after his death.

We can die with the same confidence. Since Jesus went before us, we do not need to die in fear. We can die in confidence. We can die in confidence knowing that once our spirits leave our bodies, we will be in Paradise. We can die in confidence knowing that once our spirits leave our bodies, our suffering will end. We can die in confidence knowing that once our spirits leave our bodies, we will be with the redeemed of all the ages.

When the centurion saw all that had taken place, he said, "Certainly this was a righteous man." He knew Jesus had done nothing worthy of death; he saw Jesus as innocent. He knew there was something different about Jesus, for what had just occurred does not happen when just anyone dies. He stood in awe of Jesus' death.

Just as this centurion stood in awe and wonder of Jesus' death, we need to do the same. We should be amazed that God loved us so much. Why, when we are so sinful, would God give his only Son to die for us? Why would Jesus go to the cross and not call for twelve legions of angels to rescue him? The cross stands as an amazing feat—God became flesh and died for his creatures.

People's hearts churn daily. A driver hits a dog and then sees a little boy running to hold that dying dog in his arms, and his eyes melt to tears. A parent sees a child weep because his favorite toy is broken to pieces, and his heart aches. Why is it that we are moved by such trivial matters, but remain unmoved over the death of Jesus?

The death of Jesus should cause us to live righteously. He "bore our sins in His own body on the tree, that we, having died to sins, might live for righteousness" (1 Peter 2:24). Since Jesus died for us, we need to renounce sin and embrace righteousness. Since Jesus' life was characterized by righteousness and he died for us, our lives need to be characterized by righteousness.

Will you be moved by Jesus' death? Will your life be characterized by righteousness because Jesus died for you?

Thought Questions

16. Why does Jesus' death need to be firmly fixed in our minds?

17. Does the fact that the Romans put criminals to death by crucifixion change your thinking of Jesus' experience? If so, how?

18. What does Jesus' prayer of forgiveness reveal about his character?

19. What significance does the thief's salvation have for us?

20. How do we find salvation in the cross today?

21. What was so different when Jesus died?

22. What is the significance of the temple's veil being torn in two?

23. How differently will you live because Jesus died for you?

CHAPTER FOUR:

Surely This Was the Son of God

Gandhi asked a group of Christian missionaries to sing a song representative of Christianity. The missionaries put their heads together, thought, and then began to sing, "When I Survey the Wondrous Cross." To these Christians, Jesus' cross stood as the supreme event in Christianity. The cross overshadows every other event, every other teaching in Christianity, according to these missionaries.

Indeed, Jesus' cross serves as the crux of Christianity. Without the cross, there would be no Christianity. There would be no remission of sins. There would be no hope after death. There would be no church. There would be no reason for living. But, Jesus did die—there is Christianity, there is remission of sins, there is hope after death, there is a church, there is a reason for living.

I wish I could go back in time and watch the events at Golgotha. I wish I could watch the soldiers place Jesus on the cross. I wish I could watch him writhe in agony. I wish I could watch him die. I firmly believe that if I could go back and watch Jesus on the cross, my life would be radically different. When tempted to sin, my mind would re-create the images I saw. I would more easily resist Satan, for I would fully comprehend what Jesus did for me.

Although I yearn to watch Jesus die, several people actually stood at the cross and saw what transpired. The soldiers watched him die. The Jewish leaders watched him die. His mother Mary watched him die. In this chapter, we will focus on one group who watched Jesus die—the centurion and those with him. "So when the centurion and those with him, who were guarding Jesus, saw the earthquake and the things that had happened, they feared greatly, saying, 'Truly this was the Son of God!'" (Matthew 27:54).

Just what did this group of men see that caused them to exclaim that Jesus was God's Son? We, of course, cannot get into their minds to know exactly why they said this. But, we can examine the Scriptures to see what they saw. In this chapter, we will do just that. We will investigate what these men saw so that we, too, may exclaim, "Truly, this was the Son of God!"

They Saw Jesus Refuse the Sour Wine Mingled with Gall

"And when they had come to a place called Golgotha, that is to say, Place of a Skull, they gave Him sour wine mingled with gall to drink. But when He had tasted it, He would not drink" (Matthew 27:33–34). The soldiers gave Jesus sour wine mingled with gall, but he would not drink it. Soldiers customarily gave criminals spiked wine just before they were raised on the cross. This mixture of wine with gall and myrrh was intended to dull the sense of pain of those being crucified; this mixture calmed a man's nerves and shortened his life. Many believe this custom originated with the Jews rather than the Romans; the Jews wanted those who died by crucifixion to die with some mercy.

Jesus declined this mixture, for God willed that he suffer. Isaiah described Jesus as a "Man of sorrows and acquainted with grief" (Isaiah 53:3). "We see Jesus, who was made a little lower than the angels, for the suffering of death crowned with glory and honor" (Hebrews 2:9). "Christ also suffered once for sins" (1 Peter 3:18). God did not desire that Jesus die in peace and calm. Rather, he willed that he suffer, that he take our sins and endure the punishment that should have been ours. What a Savior to refuse an anesthetic and suffer for man's sins!

Jesus, too, probably declined this mixture so his mind would be clear while he died for man. You've taken painkillers, and you know how they obscure your thinking. Jesus wanted a clear mind so that he could think of us whom he was dying to save. Jesus wished to know fully what he was doing. This clear mind allowed him to pray for the forgiveness of those crucifying him and save the thief hanging next to him.

The centurion and those with him had to be struck by this. Any normal person would have accepted these drugs that could ease his torment. Who in his right mind would not want something to alleviate his suffering? Not Jesus. Because he was the Son of God, he refused these drugs. He refused them so that he could suffer for you. He refused them so that he could think of you while he died for you.

They Saw Darkness Over the Whole Land

"Now from the sixth hour until the ninth hour there was darkness over all the land" (Matthew 27:45). For three hours—from noon until three in the afternoon—darkness covered the whole land. Some have hypothesized that a solar eclipse transpired while Jesus was on the cross. However, this cannot be, for the moon was always full on the first day of the Passover; solar eclipses cannot occur while the moon is full. This had to be a supernatural occurrence.

Whether this supernatural occurrence happened over the entire globe, or simply over Palestine, is uncertain, for the same expression would have been used for either meaning. Whether this darkness covered the whole earth or just all of Palestine does not affect the meaning of the text. The centurion and his companions found Jesus to be extraordinary, for the sun hid all its brightness. When was the last time the sun hid its glories when someone you knew died? That simply does not occur. This showed Jesus to be extraordinary.

Darkness seemed to be typical of the powers of evil that presumably were prevailing on this Friday afternoon. When the soldiers nailed Jesus to the cross, Jesus' disciples believed that the Messiah had been defeated; their messianic expectations were dashed. The Son of God was being crucified; surely he was defeated. Wasn't he?

But, this darkness may also represent the great hour of darkness that prevailed over the world. Man's sins caused the Son of God to be nailed to a cross. That's depravity and darkness in the extreme. No wonder the sun ceased to shine!

The centurion had to be awestruck by this display. He had seen people crucified before, and he saw everything continue as before. People died every day on crosses; the sun never hid its brightness. But, on this day, when this extraordinary man died, extraordinary events occurred.

They Saw Jesus Speak Forgiveness

Jesus spoke forgiveness for those who were crucifying him. From the cross, he said, "Father, forgive them, for they do not know what they do" (Luke 23:34). Although only Luke mentions this prayer, the petition conforms to what we know of Jesus' life. In his gospel, Luke goes to great lengths to show the graciousness of Jesus, and here he records just how gracious Jesus was. This prayer is in accord with Jesus' teachings—"I say to you, love your enemies" (Matthew 5:44). Isaiah prophesied of this event when he wrote the Suffering Servant "made intercession for the transgressors" (Isaiah 53:12). Jesus came to offer himself as a sacrifice for sins. Through offering himself as a sacrifice for sin, he is able to forgive even those who crucified him.

Those who crucified Jesus did not understand what they did. The New Testament teaches this. Peter told the Jews, "I know that you did it in ignorance, as did also your rulers" (Acts 3:17). "Had they known [what they were doing], they would not have crucified the Lord of glory" (1 Corinthians 2:8). Although ignorance does not excuse sin (Acts 17:30), their ignorance may have mitigated their sin.

If Jesus could forgive those who crucified him, he can forgive us of any sin we commit. "Therefore let it be known to you, brethren, that through this Man is preached to you the forgiveness of sins; and by Him everyone who believes is justified from all things from which you could not be justified by the law of Moses" (Acts 13:38–39). "In whom we have redemption through His blood, the forgiveness of sins" (Colossians 1:14). When Peter told the Jews they had crucified the Messiah, they asked what they should do. He told the crowd to repent and be baptized to have their sins forgiven; Peter offered this crowd hope and forgiveness. He did not say, "You crucified God's Son. There's just no hope for you."

If God forgave those who killed his Son, he can forgive you, too. You have done nothing so horrible as to physically crucify God's Son. John William McGarvey visited with a woman who told him that God simply could not forgive her. Her life was so horrible, she said, that God would not even come close to forgiving her. McGarvey looked her in the eyes and said, "If God could forgive those who killed Jesus, he can forgive you, too." Indeed, he can forgive you of your sin.

The centurion and those with him recognized that Jesus was different. Ordinary men would be cursing and swearing at those who killed them. They would, if it were possible, call down God's most fierce judgment, yet God's Son asked God to forgive those who nailed him to the cross. What a different crucifixion! What a wonderful Savior!

Jesus also spoke forgiveness to the thief on the cross. After the thief asked Jesus to remember him when he came into his kingdom, Jesus told him, "Assuredly, I say to you, today you will be with Me in Paradise" (Luke 23:43).

The Persians used the term "Paradise" to speak of a beautiful, walled garden. When a Persian king wished to bestow a special honor upon one of his subjects, he made him a companion in the garden. Being a companion in the garden meant this subject could walk in the garden with the king. Persians vied for the honor of walking with their king in Paradise.

Although the term occurs elsewhere in the New Testament as a synonym for heaven, we know "Paradise" does not mean that here. Jesus did not go immediately to heaven when he died. After the resurrection, he told Mary Magdalene, "Do not cling to Me, for I have not yet ascended to My Father" (John 20:17). Peter quotes David who spoke about Jesus—"You will not leave my soul in Hades" (Acts 2:27). "Hades" to the Greeks literally was the "unseen." The Greeks referred to the abode of the dead as "Hades," for the dead souls were invisible, unseen. The Paradise to which

Jesus took this penitent thief was Abraham's bosom where Lazarus dwelt after his death (Luke 16:19–31).

This gives hope for deathbed conversion. As long as a person has the breath of life in him, he can come to Jesus; it's never too late, as long as one lives. Yet, waiting to come to Jesus until one is on the deathbed is far from wise. "Behold, now is the accepted time; behold, now is the day of salvation" (2 Corinthians 6:2). We can say we're going to obey Jesus, but never do so. Felix told Paul, "Go away for now; when I have a convenient time I will call for you" (Acts 24:25). As far as we know, Felix never found that "convenient time." So many are on their deathbeds before they know what happened—a car accident takes one's life, a heart attack brings a quick death, or a disease that starts out minor become serious and one quickly dies.

Many claim that because the thief did not here receive baptism that baptism has nothing to do with salvation. A problem arises, for the New Testament teaches that one absolutely must be baptized to be saved. After his resurrection, Jesus told his disciples, "He who believes and is baptized will be saved" (Mark 16:16). When those at Pentecost realized they had crucified the Messiah and cried out for hope, Peter told them, "Repent, and let every one of you be baptized in the name of Jesus Christ for the remission of sins" (Acts 2:38). In his first epistle, Peter compares baptism to the flood in Noah's day. He says that just as eight people were saved through the waters of the flood, people today are saved through the waters of baptism (1 Peter 3:20–21).

What are we to make of this thief who received salvation but did not receive baptism? One needs to understand it cannot be proven that the thief was never baptized, for John the Baptist immersed many. One does not need to stretch the imagination too far to realize this thief may have been baptized by John. He could have turned to a life of crime following his baptism. This conjecture does not prove the thief was plunged in the Jordan, but it does raise the possibility.

One also needs to understand Jesus did not teach the multitudes the essentiality of baptism. In fact, Jesus did not baptized anyone (John 4:2). Except with the veiled reference to Nicodemus concerning one's being born of water and the Spirit, the New Testament does not record Jesus teaching anything about baptism until after his resurrection. He told his disciples to baptize new disciples "in the name of the Father and of the Son and of the Holy Spirit" (Matthew 28:19). Mark records that Jesus connected faith and baptism to salvation (Mark 16:16), yet he only did so moments before he ascended into heaven. Although Jesus may have taught about baptism—see Paul's quotation of Jesus not recorded in the Gospels in Acts 20:35—the Gospels do not record any teaching before the resurrection except to Nicodemus.

Why did Jesus not teach much about baptism in his ministry if baptism is the point when one receives salvation? Could it be that the baptism God now requires came into effect only on the first Pentecost following the death, resurrection, and ascension of Jesus? When the multitudes assembled at Pentecost realized that they had killed the Son of God, they cried out in horror as to what they could do in light of such a grievous sin. Peter told them, "Repent, and let every one of you be baptized in the name of Jesus Christ for the remission of sins" (Acts 2:38); around three thousand individuals received Christian baptism that day (Acts 2:41). As one reads through Acts, one sees that those who were converted to Jesus accepted baptism—the crowds in Samaria (Acts 8:12–13), Candace's treasurer (Acts 8:38), Saul of Tarsus (Acts 9:18; 22:16), Cornelius and those in his home (Acts 10:47–48), Lydia and those in her home (Acts 16:14–15), and the jailer in Philippi (Acts 16:33).

Another reason Jesus did not require this thief to be baptized was that while he was on earth, Jesus had the authority to forgive sins. To Pharisees and teachers of the law, Jesus said, "The Son of Man has power on earth to forgive sins" (Luke 5:24); to prove he had such power, he healed the paralytic whom he had forgiven (Luke 5:24–25). When Jesus was on this earth, he could do what he wanted—he healed the sick, he helped the lame walk, and he raised the dead—but he doesn't do that anymore. Why should we be surprised he doesn't save people without baptism anymore?

Jesus will save you. Jesus "loved us and washed us from our sins in His own blood" (Revelation 1:5). "We believe that through the grace of the Lord Jesus Christ we shall be saved' (Acts 15:11). But, this salvation comes only to those who obey Jesus—"He became the author of eternal salvation to all who obey Him" (Hebrews 5:9). Have you obeyed Jesus to receive your salvation?

Legend has it that as a bright physician in England began to succumb to a fatal disease, he searched throughout the country for one who could save his life. He finally found a doctor in London who had a good reputation. The doctor examined his patient and said, "Friend, I'm afraid the only one who can save you is Dr. Darwin of Derby." The patient replied, "But, I am Dr. Darwin of Derby!" No matter how good or righteous we are, we cannot save ourselves. We needed Jesus to do that.

The centurion and those with him realized that Jesus had to be God's Son, for only God's Son could forgive sins.

They Heard What Jesus Said When He Died

Jesus cried out with a loud voice and died. When the centurion saw that he cried out in this way, he said, "Truly this Man was the Son of God!" (Mark 15:37–39). Mark makes no mention of what Jesus said, but Luke does record the cry. Just before Jesus breathed his last, he said, "Father, 'into Your hands I commit My spirit'" (Luke 23:46). Jesus could put his faith and confidence in God. He did not have to worry about his death or his soul; he knew that God would graciously take care of him.

We can have this same confidence. Jesus released "those who through fear of death were all their lifetime subject to bondage" (Hebrews 2:15). Imagine being held in bondage by the fear of death—not knowing if you would be raised again, not knowing whether good or evil awaited you beyond the grave, not knowing if you would be reunited with loved ones who died in Jesus. Jesus came and dispelled that fear. Just as he died in confidence, and we know that Jesus will raise our mortal bodies, that good awaits the faithful beyond the grave, and that the faithful shall dwell together in bliss, so we can commit our souls to God.

During the Civil War, a Union soldier fell gravely wounded on the battlefield. His mangled body was moved from the battlefield to a hospital where no one gave him much hope for survival. A doctor examined him and told him the only way he could live was to have an operation. "But," the doctor said, "I must tell you the odds of survival are scarce. Is there anything you wish to say?"

"Get on with the operation, Doctor," the soldier replied. "If the operation is successful and I live, my mother will welcome me. If I die, Jesus will welcome me!"

Since Jesus died in our place at Golgotha, we can face death with the same confidence as this soldier. If we die, Jesus will welcome us. Do you have that confidence? Will Jesus welcome you?

Do you have this confidence? Do you know that you have a home in heaven?

Because of what the centurion and those with him saw, they exclaimed, "Surely, this was the Son of God!" Indeed he was—he lived and died as no other! No other person would have refused the spiked wine intended to calm his nerves before torture. No other person's death caused the sun to hide her face. No other person can offer salvation to one dying beside him. No other person could commit his soul to God were it not for Jesus.

Looking at the cross of Jesus, we see the Son of God. We see One who suffered for man, One at whose death the sun ceased to shine, One who spoke forgiveness for those who killed him, and One who committed his soul to God. Ordinary men do not die this way, but Jesus did. Truly, he was the Son of God.

Thought Questions

24. Why is the cross so central to Christianity?

25. Why did Jesus not drink the mixture of sour wine and gall?

26. Why could the darkness at Jesus' death not have resulted from a solar eclipse?

27. Explain why the sun might have ceased shining while Jesus died.

28. How does Jesus' plea for forgiveness harmonize with Jesus' teachings?

29. How do you know Jesus can forgive us regardless of what we've done?

30. Explain how the thief on the cross could have been saved without baptism.

31. Why might Jesus' dying words have surprised the centurion and those with him?

CHAPTER FIVE:

The Blood of the Lamb

The Death Angel prepared to make his journey through Egypt and slay the Egyptians' firstborn males. As the Angel was preparing to make this journey, Moses instructed the Israelites to place lamb's blood on their doorposts; the blood would prevent the Death Angel from slaying the firstborn in every home. The night the Death Angel would go through Egypt, great anticipation went through Israelite homes. They knew many Egyptians would die that evening and that soon, very soon, they would be leaving for the Promised Land.

As he was preparing for bed, a firstborn son asked his father to make sure the blood was in its appointed place. "Don't worry about it, honey," the father replied, "your brother put the blood on the doorpost a little while ago." "But, Dad, let's just be certain that Aaron put it there." "Ok." Father and son went to check the doorpost, but no blood could be found. Quickly, the father applied the blood to the post, and the son slept easily that evening.

That apocryphal story illustrates an important point—when God desires blood, the blood is extremely important. One has no hope without the blood of Jesus. "In that day a fountain shall be opened for the house of David and for the inhabitants of Jerusalem, for sin and for uncleanness" (Zechariah 13:1).

Jesus did indeed shed his blood. Pilate scourged Jesus (Matthew 27:26; Mark 15:15). When a man was flogged, he had to endure at least thirty-nine lashes, but he often received more. When a criminal underwent flogging, the soldier removed the clothing and bound the malefactor to a post. The soldier stretched the criminal on the post to tighten the back and make the beating easier. Soldiers used leather straps with metal balls or pieces of bone woven into them to rip the flesh. One was flogged from the shoulders to the back to the buttocks to the back of the legs. These beatings often left muscles and bones exposed. Without a doubt, Jesus lost much blood through his flogging. In fact, many died from the floggings without even making it to the cross.

When the soldiers embedded the crown of thorns on Jesus' scalp, blood must have flowed. When nails were driven through his hands and feet, Jesus certainly lost blood. As Jesus' open back scraped the cross as he tried to breathe, he must have lost blood. When a soldier pierced Jesus' side, blood and water flowed out (John 19:34).

In this lesson, we want to examine the importance of Jesus' blood and the functions of his blood.

Jesus' Blood Forgives Sins

Sin stands as man's greatest problem. No one is without sin. "There is none who does good, No, not one" (Psalm 14:3). "There is not a just man on earth who does good And does not sin" (Ecclesiastes 7:20). Man's sin alienates him from God. "If I regard iniquity in my heart, The Lord will not hear" (Psalm 66:18). "You have hidden Your face from us, And have consumed us because of our iniquities" (Isaiah 64:7). Because man sins, he stands condemned and needs a Savior.

Jesus' blood removes the sin alienating man and God. At the Last Supper, Jesus gave a cup to his disciples and said, "This is My blood of the new covenant, which is shed for many for the remission of sins" (Matthew 26:28). "Remission" indicates a pardon, the cancellation of a debt; Jesus shed his blood to pardon the sinner. "If we walk in the light as He is in the light, we have fellowship with one another, and the blood of Jesus Christ His Son cleanses us from all sin" (1 John 1:7). Jesus "washed us from our sins in His own blood" (Revelation 1:5). The great multitude in Revelation had "washed their robes and made them white in the blood of the

Lamb" (Revelation 7:14).

God could save man no other way than through Jesus' blood. Jesus asked the Father to find another way, but no other way was found. Scripture teaches that one cannot be saved without the shedding of blood. "Without shedding of blood, there is no remission" (Hebrews 9:22). "It is not possible that the blood of bulls and goats could take away sins" (Hebrews 10:4).

A learned theologian suffered from a perilous illness; his life hung in the balance. He called upon one of his most beloved students for consolation. The pupil did not know what to say to reassure such a scholarly educator. "What!" shouted the scholar. "Are you a divinity student and can you not provide some comfort at such a time?" The student spoke the text: "The blood of Jesus Christ His Son cleanses us from all sin." "That is the very word I want," said the teacher, and he dismissed his student. When life hangs in the balance, we can take comfort in the certainty that Jesus' blood cleanses us from sin.

Have you been in contact with Jesus' blood? Do you have the remission of sins?

Jesus' Blood Brings the New Testament

The Old Covenant laid a heavy burden upon those who attempted to follow the Law. Peter called the Old Testament a yoke "which neither our fathers nor we were able to bear" (Acts 15:10). Paul spoke of the Law's being "contrary to us" (Colossians 2:14). The Old Testament contained many regulations, and no one—save Jesus—came close to keeping them perfectly. Thus, the New Testament writers spoke of the Law being contrary to us and a heavy burden to bear.

Although the Old Testament exacted a heavy toll upon those to whom it was given, the Mosaic Code perfectly served its intended purpose. The Law revealed sin (Romans 7:7). The Old Covenant demonstrated that sin must be punished. Take, for example, blasphemy against Yahweh—whoever spoke evil against the Lord was to be stoned to death (Leviticus 24:16). The Old Testament also exposed the need for a Savior. Once a year, the high priest made atonement for himself and for the people (Leviticus 16); the priest and the nation needed such atonement, for no one thoroughly kept the Law.

When Jesus died at Golgotha, he removed the Old Testament as the way man honored God; he established the New Covenant as the way man serves God. When Jesus established the Lord's Supper as a way for his children to remember him, he told his disciples, "This is My blood of the new covenant" (Matthew 26:28; see also 1 Corinthians 11:25). Jeremiah prophesied that God would establish a new covenant: "Behold, the days are coming, says the Lord, when I will make a new covenant with the house of Israel and with the house of Judah" (Jeremiah 31:31). Jesus "abolished in His flesh the enmity, that is, the law of commandments contained in ordinances" (Ephesians 2:15). Jesus "wiped out the handwriting of requirements that was against us, which was contrary to us. And He has taken it out of the way, having nailed it to the cross" (Colossians 2:14).

Because Jesus nailed the Law to his cross, we no longer abide by the Old Law. We no longer sacrifice animals, for Jesus gave himself. We no longer circumcise male infants, for baptism serves as a spiritual circumcision (Colossians 2:11–12). We no longer need a separate priesthood, for all Christians serve as priests (1 Peter 2:9). We no longer need a Levitical high priest, for Jesus ministers as our High Priest (Hebrews 8:1).

Jesus' Blood Redeems

The New Testament teaches that Jesus redeemed the church with his blood. Paul told the Ephesian elders: "Shepherd the church of God which *He purchased with His own blood*" (Acts 20:28, emphasis mine). We were redeemed "with the precious blood of Christ, as of a lamb without blemish and without spot" (1 Peter 1:19). "In Him we have redemption through His blood, the forgiveness of sins, according to the riches of His grace" (Ephesians 1:7). "In whom we have redemption through His blood, the forgiveness of sins" (Colossians 1:14). "You are worthy to take the scroll, And to open its seals; For You were slain, And have redeemed us to God by Your blood Out of every tribe and tongue and people and nation" (Revelation 5:9).

Redemption implies deliverance by payment of a price. In other words, sin held man captive and God paid a heavy price for man's freedom. God paid that costly price with the blood of his Son.

A young boy lived along the Mississippi River. Each day, he watched as large ships moved up and down the river. One afternoon, his father came home somewhat later than usual. As his father walked through the door, he handed Andy a box. Andy opened the box and inside was a model ship in pieces. Andy worked tirelessly that evening to build his ship. Finally, he finished the ship, set it on a shelf, and went to bed, all the while anticipating taking his new boat down to the river after school the next day.

As Andy sat in school the next day, the hours crept by. He couldn't wait to get home and sail his ship. Finally, the final bell rang and Andy, barely touching the ground, ran all the way home. He burst through the door, threw his books on his bed, grabbed his boat, and made a dash to the river. He gently placed his boat in the water and watched it sail. Andy sailed his little boat for hours. But, as he was preparing to return home, a speedboat came barging down the river. Andy's boat became caught up in the waves generated by the speedboat and it quickly got away from him. Andy stood and watched in horror as his ship was swept down the river.

Andy returned home while his tears watered the pavement. As he lay in bed, all he could think was: "My boat is lost! My boat is lost!" Every day for months, Andy returned to the river to see if his boat had been washed ashore. But, he always returned home empty handed. One day, as he came home from school, he noticed his boat in a store window. He ran in and told the clerk, "That's my boat. My daddy bought it for me and I made it. It became lost on the river." The clerk told Andy the boat would cost him two dollars. Andy pleaded with the clerk to give him his boat, but his pleading proved fruitless.

Andy ran home, busted his piggy bank, collected two dollars, and returned to the store. He placed his eight quarters on the counter, and the clerk handed him his boat. As Andy walked home, he looked at that model ship and said, "You are twice mine. Once because I made you, and once because I bought you."

That's reconciliation. That's what Jesus did for us. He made us, and when we were enslaved to Satan, he bought us. We are twice his.

Jesus' Blood Justifies

Jesus' blood justifies sinners. "Much more then, having now been justified by His blood, we shall be saved from wrath through Him" (Romans 5:9). Justification takes place when God declares that sinners are righteous before him. Because of Jesus' work, sinners can stand right in God's sight. Had Jesus not come and offered his blood, there would be no way for man to stand right before God. Yet, through his blood, we stand right before him.

Through the blood of Jesus, God sees his children as perfect. Not because we are sinless, for our sins are many. But, God sees us as perfect through the blood of Jesus. As God looks at us, he does so through "blood-colored glasses." Through those "glasses," we stand faultless before God's throne. No wonder Jude praised Jesus as the one who could present us faultless before the throne of God (Jude 24).

During the Second World War, a young man, out of patriotism, joined the army. He really wanted to see some action during the war, and in a search for action, he went AWOL. However, he was caught and sentenced to seven years in prison. The judge suspended his prison sentence and told him, "As long as you remain in the military, you will not see a day in prison. But, if you leave the army before your term is up, you will spend the remainder of your term in prison." This soldier was released from the army before his seven years were up, and he went to the prosecutor's office to see where he would be forced to spend the rest of his sentence. To his great delight, he discovered that President Truman had granted him a full pardon. The prosecutor told the private, "This means your record is clear. It is as though you had never been convicted of a crime."

That is the way justification works. Because of Jesus' blood, we stand before God as though we have never sinned. Our records have been cleared. Does God see you through the blood of Jesus? Have you been justified in his sight? Is your record clear?

Jesus' Blood Sanctifies

Jesus' blood sanctifies sinners. The author of Hebrews calls it "the blood of the covenant by which [we were] sanctified" (Hebrews 10:29). "Jesus also, that He might sanctify the people with His own blood, suffered outside the gate" (Hebrews 13:12).

Sanctification represents separating the believer from sin and dedicating him to God's own righteousness. The blood of Jesus makes us holy. We stand holy before God, not because of our own holiness, but because the blood of Jesus sanctifies us.

Since Jesus' blood has sanctified us, we need to live sanctified lives. To the sexually immoral in Thessalonica, Paul wrote: "This is the will of God, your sanctification" (1 Thessalonians 4:3). Our lives need to be marked by holiness, devotion to God, and doing good. Since Jesus in his blood has sanctified us—separated us from sin, made us holy—how can we live in sin? Isn't that exactly what Scripture teaches? "What shall we say then? Shall we continue in sin that grace may abound? Certainly not! How shall we who died to sin live any longer in it?" (Romans 6:1–2).

Indeed, how can we live in sin after we've been sanctified in Jesus' blood? Jesus left heaven, and all of its splendor, and came to this earth to give his blood whereby we could be sanctified. Why spurn the blood by which we were sanctified? Why not live sanctified lives?

Jesus' Blood Allows Access to God

"Having boldness to enter the Holiest by the blood of Jesus" (Hebrews 10:19). We can go boldly to God's throne because we have been washed in Jesus' blood. We are not perfect, and when we sin, we need cleansing. To achieve that cleansing, we can go to God's throne with boldness because Jesus sprinkled us in his blood.

Great blessings await us at God's throne. In speaking of Jesus as the Christian's high priest, the writer of Hebrews said, "Let us therefore come boldly to the throne of grace, that we may obtain mercy and find grace to help in time of need" (Hebrews 4:16). We find mercy at God's throne. How we need mercy! When we dwell upon immoral thoughts, we need God's mercy. When we become angry and say what we shouldn't, we need God's mercy. When we give ourselves so much to our work that we have no time for family, we need God's mercy. We find the mercy we need at the throne of God. We can go to the throne of God through the blood of Jesus.

When we go to the throne of God through Jesus' blood, we also find "grace to help in time of need." When we face temptation and contemplate sinning, we need God's grace to help us overcome. God gives us that grace at his throne. If we look to God, he will provide a way to avoid sinning (1 Corinthians 10:13). We find such grace, such help, through the blood of Jesus.

Those who drink Jesus' blood have eternal life (John 6:53–56). Each week, Christians take the Lord's supper and drink, in a symbolic way, Jesus' blood. Do you partake of Jesus' blood? Do you need to come in contact with Jesus' blood?

Thought Questions

32. Describe the process when Jesus shed his blood.

33. Why could God not save man except through the blood of Jesus?

34. Why did the Old Covenant need to be replaced?

35. What purposes did the Old Covenant fulfill?

36. What is meant by redemption?

37. Describe justification. Why does man need to be justified?

38. How does Jesus' blood sanctify the sinner?

39. How can the Christian go boldly before God's throne?

CHAPTER SIX:

The Greatest Death

The Christian knows that death can be a blessing. When a believer's body has been overtaken by disease and he goes to be with the Lord, the Christian relative grieves, but he does so with hope. He knows that although he will miss his loved one, his family member's suffering has ceased. He has confidence that his loved one resides safely in Jesus' arms. The Christian anticipates seeing his loved one again when Jesus returns and raises the dead. "'Blessed are the dead who die in the Lord from now on.' 'Yes,' says the Spirit, 'that they may rest from their labors, and their works follow them'" (Revelation 14:13).

When my grandfather left this world, I saw firsthand how death can be a blessing. Cancer had eaten his body. His pain had become unbearable; he was too weak to swallow pain medication. My grandmother cared for him around the clock. He finally slipped from this life to dwell in the city of God. His death came as a blessing, not because we do not miss him, but because he died in the Lord. His suffering ended, and he now has bliss beyond compare.

As blessed as death can be for the Christian, Jesus' death serves as the greatest blessing. His death stands as a tremendous blessing for the world. His death paves the way for men to leave sin and serve God. His death allows men to die in confidence of living with

God. In this chapter, we examine Jesus' death and how his death blesses the world.

Christ's Death Was For Us

"For when we were still without strength, in due time Christ died for the ungodly. For scarcely for a righteous man will one die; yet perhaps for a good man someone would even dare to die. But God demonstrates His own love toward us, in that while we were still sinners, Christ died for us" (Romans 5:6–8). Christ died for us when we had no strength. He died for us while we were sick, feeble, and weak. In this specific context, the term for "without strength" carries a connotation of "helplessness." Before Jesus died, we were helpless. Without Jesus' death, we could not have salvation; regardless of what we did, we would be lost. The salvation we do have comes through Jesus. Jesus himself said, "I am the way, the truth, and the life. No one comes to the Father except through Me" (John 14:6). Peter, speaking of Jesus, declared, "There is no other name under heaven given among men by which we must be saved" (Acts 4:12).

What if Jesus had not died for man? There would be no hope. Imagine your doctor calling to say cancer was devouring your body. Getting off the telephone, you'd know there was nothing to grasp onto. You'd be leaving your family and friends, but you would be doing so with no possibility of seeing them again. There would be nothing beyond the grave to give hope. You would be dying and nothing, absolutely nothing, could provide solace.

But, Jesus' death, while "we were still without strength," provides solace. Although we know this life will shortly end, we know that a new life will shortly begin. We know that, although we will leave friends and loved ones, we shall be reunited with them at Jesus' feet. We know that as life leaves our bodies, we shall be together with God. Life beyond the grave provides great hope.

Christ died for man in due time. Jesus came and died for man at just the right time; Paul made this point elsewhere: "When the fullness of time had come, God sent forth His Son" (Galatians 4:4). God, through his providence, prepared the world to receive the Christ. The *Pax Romana* (Roman Peace) allowed Christian missionaries to move freely without threat of war. Roman defeat caused many tribal peoples to lose faith in their local deities because these idols failed to prevent overthrow by the Romans; this left people with a sense of longing for a true God to worship. Elaborate roads made travel within the Roman Empire easy. Greek had become the universal language; the apostles and their companions wrote the New Testament in Greek. The universality of Greek allowed the gospel to spread readily.

God did not send Christ into this world haphazardly. Jesus came when this world was ready. Great planning went into Jesus' death. This demonstrates the depth of the Father's love. He cared for man so much that he made sure the world situation allowed for the spread of the gospel. When his Son died, God wanted the whole world to know what he had done. He wanted the whole world to have the possibility of escaping sin and living with him. He wanted the gospel to spread readily.

The gospel needed to spread readily, for Christ died for the ungodly. When man lives in sin, he is the opposite of everything God is; hence, the term "ungodly." The ungodly stand to receive God's strictest judgment. The world has been "reserved for fire until the day of judgment and perdition of ungodly men" (2 Peter 3:7). Before Christ came to die for the ungodly, we stood to receive God's judgment and perdition.

Men generally do not die for one another. Scarcely will a man die for a self-righteous man, who does what the law requires. He abides by the law, but he shows no kindness or mercy. He refuses to do what the law does not require. Few, very few, men would die for such a man.

But, one might die for a good person. The good man does more than just what is right in the law's eyes—he also shows kindness and mercy. He willingly gives of himself. He genuinely loves people and strives to help. A few men might die for such a person.

On some occasions, men have died for others. Men have bravely gone to war, and were willing to sacrifice their lives, if need be, to protect the rights of others. Stories from Nazi concentration camps tell how one prisoner would willingly die to save another. The men and women aboard United Airlines Flight 93 on

September 11, 2001, brought down the plane to save as many as possible on the ground. Although a host of men have died for others, their deaths form the exception rather than the rule.

God demonstrates his love toward man through Jesus' unusual, sacrificial death. If a man does not exhibit love, can we say he has love at all? If a husband never showed any affection, never brought home flowers, never took her to dinner, his wife would rightly conclude that he did not love her. We show love through our actions. God, too, demonstrates his love through his actions. He proved his love for man through Jesus' death—he could have allowed man to be lost instead of sacrificing his Son. What would God have lost had he allowed man to be damned? I have two sons, and nothing in this world would cause me to voluntarily give their lives for others. God did the unthinkable—he gave his Son to die for man.

God proved his love in that Jesus died for man while man still lived in sin. Jesus died even as man disregarded God's holiness. In reading the New Testament, one learns that many people of that time period worshiped idols rather than the true God. Many others lived selfishly, without regard to what God wanted in their lives.

This continues to be true today. Many throughout the world disregard God's holiness through paganism—Islam, Buddhism, Hinduism, and other non-Christian religions dominate the world scene. Within Christendom, many disregard the Scriptures to serve God in their own ways. Others live as they choose without thought to God; they seek power or money; they lie; they are sexually promiscuous. They live this way because they deny the existence of God, they believe he will overlook their sin, or they seek their own self-interests.

These are the ones for whom Christ died. Granted, he died for the little lady who has served God as faithfully as possible her entire life. But, he also died for those who live in gross sin. He died for the child molesters, he died for the drug addicts, and he died for the mass murderers. He died for them to provide them the liberty of coming to him.

Jesus' death for the ungodly shows God's overwhelming love. Who, in his natural inclination, would give to those who misuse him? Who would give to those who misused his son? Parents often protect their children more than they protect themselves. If you want to see me angry, mistreat one of my sons. Yet, God sent his Son to suffer torture, to be mistreated, and to be killed for man's redemption.

Who would die for his chief enemies? Each of us has enemies—neighbors who throw trash on our lawns; coworkers who, seeking our jobs, go to our bosses with false reports; those who always have to make some cutting remarks. Who among us really wants to do good for our enemies? But that is exactly what Christ did—he died for his enemies.

Jesus' death for the ungodly also shows God's overwhelming hatred for sin. Sin is so destructive that Jesus had to be crucified to remove sin. When we are tempted, we would do well to remember God's hatred for sin and Christ's suffering for it. Jesus endured the torture of the cross to free us from sin. When we sin, we are rendering Christ's sacrifice useless and we are stirring up God's hatred.

Jesus died "for us," for our benefit, on our behalf. His death does us good. Jesus' death benefits us in that we should have died instead of him. He took the punishment upon himself that should have been ours. His death benefits us by paving the way for our salvation.

In Arizona, an Indian newlywed was plowing corn while his bride worked inside their mud hut. In the course of her work, the young girl turned over a rock and a rattlesnake crawled out. The snake coiled up and bit her. The young lady screamed loudly, and her husband came running back from the field. Once inside their home, the young man killed the snake and squeezed his bride's leg tightly. He sucked the poison from the wound, thus saving his wife's life. However, he had a small sore on his mouth that allowed the venom to enter his bloodstream. He died shortly thereafter.

That's exactly what Jesus did for us. He died in our place. It is we who should have died. But, Jesus stepped forward and offered himself in our stead. What an amazing demonstration of God's love for man!

Christ's Death Benefits Us

"Much more then, having now been justified by His blood, we

shall be saved from wrath through Him. For if when we were enemies we were reconciled to God through the death of His Son, much more, having been reconciled, we shall be saved by His life. And not only that, but we also rejoice in God through our Lord Jesus Christ, through whom we have now received the reconciliation" (Romans 5:9–11). Jesus' blood provides for our justification. Justification refers to the process in which God declares the sinner innocent. The sinner is not innocent by himself; his innocence comes through the blood of Jesus. Being justified by faith gives us peace with God (Romans 5:1). The blood of bulls and goats could never take away sin (Hebrews 10:4). However, the blood of Jesus can (and does) take away sin.

We shall be saved from wrath through Jesus. God's wrath will come upon the world. A cursory reading of Scripture shows that God will send his judgment—"The wrath of God is revealed from heaven against all ungodliness and unrighteousness of men" (Romans 1:18); "The wrath of God comes upon the sons of disobedience" (Ephesians 5:6). God will execute swift and terrible wrath upon the world. The first time God poured out his wrath upon the world, he did so with water—every living being died, save Noah and his family. God promised that the next time he executes wrath upon the world, he will do so with fire.

The New Testament paints glimpses of this wrath. The Lord Jesus will come from heaven "in flaming fire taking vengeance" on the disobedient who will be "punished with everlasting destruction from the presence of the Lord and from the glory of His power" (2 Thessalonians 1:7–9). The author of Hebrews gave this warning: "It is a fearful thing to fall into the hands of the living God" (Hebrews 10:31). The rich man was being tormented in fire, so much so that he desired just a drop of water on his tongue (Luke 16:24). Those in hell "have no rest day or night" (Revelation 14:11).

Through Jesus' death, Christians shall be saved from this wrath. When God's wrath comes upon the world, Christians shall stand safe, for Jesus took their wrath upon himself.

Those in the western United States often faced wildfires. If a man noticed a wildfire approaching, he might burn a large area of earth, allowing the fire to be extinguished before the wildfire could

The Greatest Death

reach him. When the wildfire would approach, he would stand in the spot where he had burned the earth. He would be safe, because fire would have already consumed that plot of ground where he stood. Likewise, the Christian is safe in Jesus, because God's wrath has already consumed him.

Christians have been reconciled to God. Before Jesus died, we were God's enemies. Our sin alienated us from God. Because God dwells in absolute holiness, he had no choice but to regard sinners as his enemies. But, through Jesus' death, Christians have been reconciled, brought back into fellowship, with God. When a couple has serious marital problems and separates, the husband and wife may seek a way to come back together. If they reach some kind of agreement, they are "reconciled." Because Jesus died for us, we can have a close relationship with God rather than being alienated from him.

A "hippie" in California left home because his father spoke so harshly. The father refused to have any contact with this eldest son, but the mother prayed daily for the son's return. The son refused to return home until his father would apologize and accept his political views. Years passed, and the mother contracted cancer. She made one last request of her husband: for him to call their son. He did so, and the son caught the first plane he could get. All the while refusing to speak, the father and son stood in the presence of the dying woman. With the last ounce of strength she had, she placed the hand of the son into the hand of the father, and she then died. The father looked at his wife and then looked up at his son. They fell into each other's arms with weeping.

That's reconciliation. The father and son stood estranged from one another, but through the dying act of the mother, they reconciled. In the same way, man and God stood alienated from one another because of man's sin. Through the dying act of the Son, man can be reconciled to the Father.

We shall be saved by Jesus' death. We received reconciliation through Jesus' death, and his continued life brings salvation. Jesus did not complete his work at Calvary. But, he was raised back to life and provides salvation.

Paul and those with him rejoiced in God through Jesus. We can have great rejoicing through Jesus and what he has done on our behalf. After the Ethiopian eunuch had been baptized, he went on his way rejoicing (Acts 8:39). The persecuted Christians to whom Peter wrote rejoiced "with joy inexpressible and full of glory" (1 Peter 1:18). If they could rejoice in persecution, surely Jesus can bring us joy in the midst of our lives.

Each of us shall die some day. A drunk driver might hit someone's car, or a doctor will say he can do no more. Family and friends will gather around the casket and remember the person's life. Pallbearers will carry the body from the hearse to the grave at the cemetery. Dirt will fill the grave, and a marker will be placed so loved ones can come there to mourn.

Although we shall die, we shall die in hope. Jesus Christ has gone before us. He has died for us. Therefore, we can die with full assurance. We can die with assurance of escaping God's wrath. We can die with assurance of a reunion with our loved ones. We can die with assurance of living with God in eternity. We can die with assurance, because Jesus' death is, indeed, the greatest death.

Thought Questions

40. Discuss how death can be a blessing for the Christian.

41. What did Paul mean when he wrote that Christ died for us when we were without strength?

42. In what way did Christ die for man in due time?

43. Why did Christ die for the ungodly?

44. How does man know that God loves him?

45. How does Jesus' death benefit man?

46. How shall we be saved from wrath through Jesus?

47. Describe reconciliation.

CHAPTER SEVEN:

The Good Shepherd

Many find comfort in Psalm 23: "The Lord is my shepherd; I shall not want." A friend of mine quotes this psalm every time he preaches at a funeral. Many have recited these words before going into an operating room for serious surgery. George W. Bush quoted from the psalm in his address to the nation from the Oval Office on September 11, 2001.

Although these words provide much needed comfort, the Lord being our shepherd tells only half the story. Jesus revealed the full truth when he said, "I am the good shepherd" (John 10:11). In this context, "good" means something like "noble." The Lord is, therefore, not only our shepherd; he is our noble shepherd.

In John 10, Jesus explained how he was the good shepherd. In this chapter, we explore Jesus' teaching so that we might fully understand his being the good shepherd. Jesus teaches us the good shepherd would:

Breathe His Last for His Sheep

"I am the good shepherd. The good shepherd gives His life for the sheep. But a hireling, one who is not the shepherd, one who does not own the sheep, sees the wolf coming and leaves the sheep and flees; and the wolf catches the sheep and scatters them. The hireling flees because he is a hireling and does not care about the sheep" (John 10:11–13). The good shepherd dies to protect his sheep. In antiquity, many shepherds did die while saving their flocks. David killed both a lion and a bear when they attacked his sheep (1 Samuel 17:34–36); if the Lord had not empowered David, he likely would have succumbed to the lion or bear. Amos speaks of a shepherd's rescuing "two legs or a piece of an ear" from a lion's mouth (Amos 3:12); in other words, a shepherd would pull his sheep from the mouth of a hungry lion. When most would run, the shepherd would rescue.

The sacrifice is "for" the sheep, that is, on their behalf. When he died, Jesus took our place. "He made Him who knew no sin to be sin for us, that we might become the righteousness of God in Him" (2 Corinthians 5:21). "Christ has redeemed us from the curse of the law, *having become a curse for us*" (Galatians 3:13, emphasis mine). He did so, because we could not save ourselves (Isaiah 53:5).

In the course of the First World War, some French soldiers prepared to make a grenade run through no-man's-land. Suddenly, a grenade fell to the ground with its firing pin drawn. Everyone knew the grenade would soon explode, for there was no time to discard it. Quickly one of the soldiers fell on the grenade. The grenade exploded, and the soldier died. But, he had saved the others.

The hireling, on the other hand, does not die for the sheep. Since he does not own them, the hireling does not lose his livelihood if a wolf comes and devours the sheep. The hireling sees the wolf coming and flees. He concerns himself with his own safety, not the safety of the sheep. Then the wolf comes and destroys the sheep.

Jesus could have concerned himself with his own safety. Who would not have done anything in his power to save himself from a horrible death? Jesus died willingly for man. He could have called for twelve legions of angels (Matthew 26:53). He gave his life of his own accord (v. 18). Jesus willing gave his life for the sheep (Matthew 20:28).

Befriend His Sheep

"I am the good shepherd; and I know My sheep, and am known by My own. As the Father knows Me, even so I know the Father;

and I lay down My life for the sheep" (John 10:14–15). The good shepherd knows his sheep. He knows his sheep by name (John 10:3). "The Lord knows those who are His" (2 Timothy 2:19). The Lord knows your name and he cares about you. He knows the struggles you have. He knows the hard time your co-workers give you. He knows your mother barely speaks to you because you became a Christian.

The sheep know the good shepherd. The sheep know the good shepherd's voice and they follow him (John 10:4). If we know Jesus, we will follow him. During World War I, some Turkish fighters attempted to confiscate some sheep from a Jerusalem hillside. As the shepherd was awakened from sleep, he realized his sheep were being taken away. Frantically, he contemplated a way to recapture the sheep. He did the only thing he knew to do: he cupped his hands around his mouth and gave his peculiar call the sheep heard daily. The sheep stopped. The shepherd repeated his call. The sheep turned around and ran back across the ravine to the shepherd. Nothing the soldiers attempted to do worked. The sheep knew the shepherd's voice, and they responded.

How well do we know Jesus' voice? How much time do we spend studying the Scriptures so that we can know what Jesus expects from us? How much time do we spend obeying Jesus as if we were sheep following the shepherd?

Bring Together His Sheep

"And other sheep I have which are not of this fold; them also I must bring, and they will hear My voice; and there will be one flock and one shepherd" (John 10:16). Jesus had other sheep who were not of the fold to whom he was speaking. When examining the context, one quickly realizes "this fold" refers to the Jewish people. Therefore, the "other sheep" stands for the Gentiles. Jesus here prophesied that Gentiles would be accepted in him.

By no means was Jesus the first to speak of Gentile acceptance in God's plan. Isaiah prophesied that Jesus would be a "light to the Gentiles" (Isaiah 42:6). Speaking through Isaiah, God said of Christ, "Behold! My Servant whom I uphold, My Elect One in whom My soul delights! I have put My Spirit upon Him; He will bring forth justice to the Gentiles" (Isaiah 42:1). Many nations would come into the church (Micah 4:1–5).

The good shepherd would bring Gentiles into his fold. These other sheep would hear the shepherd's voice, as would the other sheep. When this occurred, there would be one flock and one shepherd. There would no longer be two flocks, but one. This one flock would be united instead of divided. In speaking of the separation between Jews and Gentiles, Paul wrote: "For He Himself is our peace, who has made both one, and has broken down the middle wall of separation, having abolished in His flesh the enmity, that is, the law of commandments contained in ordinances, so as to create in Himself one new man from the two, thus making peace, and that He might reconcile them both to God in one body through the cross, thereby putting to death the enmity" (Ephesians 2:14–16).

Had Jesus not brought in the Gentiles, we would have no hope. We, being Gentiles, depend on God's acceptance of Gentiles for salvation. Imagine knowing that God would provide salvation for an ethnic group of which you are not a part. Imagine knowing what wonderful blessings can be found in Christ but having no way to get into Christ. Imagine being forced to follow the Mosaic Code—being forced to keep the Sabbath and to offer animal sacrifices.

All of This Benefits the Shepherd

"Therefore My Father loves Me, because I lay down My life that I may take it again. No one takes it from Me, but I lay it down of Myself. I have power to lay it down, and I have power to take it again. This command I have received from My Father" (John 10:17–18). The Father loves the good shepherd. He loves the good shepherd, because he lays down his life. The shows just how much the Father loves man. He loves man so much that he loves the one who dies for man.

No one takes the good shepherd's life. He voluntarily lays it down (Matthew 26:53). Jesus chose to die for us. He wanted to redeem us from sin. He wanted to provide us with a home in heaven.

During the Truman Administration, an attempt was made on the life of the president. In his duty to protect the president, a secret

The Good Shepherd

service officer was killed. A fund was established to assist the officer's family. President Truman helped to raise funds, and as he did so, he said, "You can't imagine just how a man feels when someone else dies for him." Jesus Christ has died for us. How do we feel? How will we respond to his love?

The good shepherd also has power to take his life back up as the Father commanded him. Jesus had the power to take his life back up again. He demonstrated this power when he came back from the grave. Because Jesus rose from the grave, he will one day raise us (1 Corinthians 15:22–23). That's the power he had to take his life back up.

Jesus had received this commandment from the Father. He obeyed the Father to the point of death (Philippians 2:8). Jesus was willing to obey the Father, even if his obedience caused his own death. His obedience ultimately resulted in his death. Because Jesus obeyed the Father, we can have eternal life.

Jesus is the good shepherd, and he loves us dearly. Won't you return that love?

Thought Questions

48. Why does Psalm 23 provide such comfort?

49. What is the significance of the good shepherd laying down his life for the sheep?

50. Why would the hireling not die for the sheep?

51. In what way does the good shepherd befriend his sheep?

52. How much significance should be placed upon Jesus bringing Gentiles into his fold?

53. Why did Jesus voluntarily die for the sheep?

54. How will you return Jesus' love?

CHAPTER EIGHT:

From the Mouth of a Dying Man

In *Richard II*, Shakespeare wrote: "O, but they say the tongues of dying men enforce attention like a deep harmony: Where words are scarce they are seldom spent in vain, for they breathe their words in pain." As life drains from a man's body, he will not use his words carelessly. He will prudently choose each word, for he knows any one of them may very well be his last. As he speaks in the last moments of life, one can learn much about him from what he says. Where will his heart be? Will he speak words of comfort and love to his family? Will he seek forgiveness for some wrong committed against his wife? Will he give a final piece of advice to his children? Will he plead with God for mercy after a life of sin?

In this chapter, we analyze Jesus' dying words. This investigation gives us a glimpse of Jesus' inner being. In coming to terms with who Jesus was, we are better able to grasp the sacrifice he made at Golgotha. This affords a greater understanding of our salvation. This will, hopefully, lead to a more righteous lifestyle.

The Gospels record seven statements Jesus made while being crucified. Some have attempted to put these sayings in chronological order, yet that task is difficult at best and yields no useful fruit. We will make no attempt to assign these statements a chronological order; we will examine these cries as they are documented in the Gospels.

Jesus Was a Forsaken Dying Man

"And about the ninth hour Jesus cried out with a loud voice, saying, 'Eli, Eli, lama sabachthani?' that is, 'My God, My God, why have You forsaken Me?'" (Matthew 27:46). These words appear in the opening of Psalm 22. That Davidic psalm minutely portrays the suffering Jesus endured on the cross. In fact, given Jesus' quote, many scholars believe Jesus may have meditated upon this psalm during the crucifixion. Whether or not Jesus meditated upon this psalm does not aid our understanding of these words. Jesus obviously found the opening of Psalm 22 suitable to his situation, so he took David's prayer and made it his own.

This cry shows the Father's abandonment of the Son. Granted, one cannot fathom how the Father forsook the Son, for the Father and Son are one (John 10:30). But, Psalm 22:3 explains why the Father left the Son; that text simply says of God, "You are holy." God dwells in absolute holiness, and the Son bore the sins of mankind. Since Jesus bore man's sins, the Father had no choice but to leave his Son to die alone. "He made Him who knew no sin to be sin for us" (2 Corinthians 5:21). "Christ has redeemed us from the curse of the law, having become a curse for us" (Galatians 3:13).

Jesus hung at Golgotha all alone. One of his disciples handed him over to the authorities. Another disciple, fearing for his own life, denied he even knew who Jesus was. All of the other disciples fled, because they suspected they, too, might be crucified. Not only did his closest friends leave him, but the Father had deserted him as well. Jesus was truly alone.

Imagine dying of cancer. Your wife never comes to see you in the hospital. Your children stay away. Your parents refuse to accept your phone calls. Your best friend never sends a card. Contemplate the loneliness! Jesus died all alone. He was not surrounded by his friends and loved ones. Even God, in whom he trusted, was not there.

Our sins caused the Father to abandon his Son; this shows just how reprehensible God finds sin. When you spend time watching questionable television, you caused the Father to leave the Son. When you tell your employer a "little white lie" to stay out of trouble, you caused the Father to leave the Son. When you're so tired on a Sunday evening that you stay home from the assembly, you caused the Father to leave the Son.

Jesus Was a Meditating Dying Man

"Jesus said, 'Father, forgive them, for they do not know what they do'" (Luke 23:34). Those who crucified Jesus did not fully comprehend what they did. Paul wrote, "Had they known [what they were doing], they would not have crucified the Lord of glory" (1 Corinthians 2:8). In asking the Father's forgiveness for those who killed him ignorantly, Jesus demonstrated that although some may sin ignorantly, they still sin. Whether or not a person understands that an act is sinful, he sins if he commits that act. Furthermore, God no longer accepts ignorance as a viable excuse for sin; although he once overlooked ignorance, he now commands "all men everywhere to repent" (Acts 17:30).

Jesus' prayer establishes that God can save anyone. If God could forgive those who nailed his Son to the cross, he can forgive you, too. Although we all have sinned, we have never taken Jesus and physically nailed him to the cross. But, those who did so could receive forgiveness. Many say that God cannot forgive them; their sins are too horrible. Yet, they could do nothing comparable with crucifying the Son of God.

Jesus' prayer puts him in the role of mediator. He is, indeed, a mediator. "There is one God and one Mediator between God and men, the Man Christ Jesus" (1 Timothy 2:5). Mediation alludes to the process of bringing two parties together. If a husband and wife separate, they may go to a neutral third party. The third party will try to help them solve their disagreements and reconcile. That's mediation. Jesus is the go-between for God and man to resolve the sin problem.

The author of Hebrews went a step further than Paul did: "He always lives to make intercession for them" (Hebrews 7:25). This very day, Jesus continues to make intercession for sinners. He stands before God's throne to intercede for his children. Are you his child? Does he intercede for you before his Father's throne?

Jesus Was a Saving Dying Man

To the penitent criminal, Jesus said, "Assuredly, I say to you, today you will be with Me in Paradise" (Luke 23:43). This remark shows that Jesus thought of others in his dying moments. As he died on the cross, Jesus was not primarily concerned with his own wellbeing. Could one say that Jesus was even concerned with himself at all? He went to the cross for the salvation of others. Here, we see Jesus saving another from the cross.

Jesus saves us today through his sacrifice at Calvary. We are redeemed by the precious blood of Christ (1 Peter 1:18–19). Christ's blood cleanses our consciences to serve the living God (Hebrews 9:14). Jesus has washed us from our sins in his blood (Revelation 1:5). If we strive to do right, "the blood of Jesus Christ His Son cleanses us from all sin" (1 John 1:7).

Several years ago, a preacher in Alabama lay on his sickbed. He had proclaimed the unsearchable riches of Christ for more than half a century. His son came into the room where he lay to say his good-byes.

The son said, "Dad, you have preached for many, many years. You have done more good than any other man I know."

The dying servant of God said, "Don't tell me that, Son. Tell me about the blood of Jesus. Nothing but the blood of Jesus will do for a dying man."

How true! Nothing but the blood of Jesus will do for a dying man. But, Jesus came and shed his blood. That blood will abundantly cover any sin we may have. We can put our confidence, not in our works, but in the blood of Jesus Christ. Can you truly say that you can put your confidence in Jesus' blood?

Jesus Was a Crying Dying Man

"And when Jesus had cried out with a loud voice, He said, 'Father, "into Your hands I commit My spirit."' Having said this, He breathed His last" (Luke 23:46). This cry shows Jesus' confidence in the Father. Since the spirit returns to God "who gave it" (Ecclesiastes 12:7), Jesus did not worry about his soul, for God would take care of him. He knew his Father would take him to Paradise; Jesus told the thief that they would be together there on that very day. Jesus had assurance of his salvation; therefore, he could confidently commit his soul to God.

As we prepare to die, we can face death with the same conviction Jesus exhibited here. Death does not need to be feared. Even in death, God cares for his children; when Lazarus died, angels carried his spirit to Abraham's bosom (Luke 16:22). God has prepared a city for his children (Hebrews 11:16).

One day, dear reader, you will die. But, how will you die? Will you be able, as Jesus did, to say, "Father, into your hands I commit my spirit"? Will you die in full assurance that God will care for you even after your death? Or, will you beg God for mercy? Will you plead for more time, because you know you stand condemned before God? Just how will you die?

Jesus Was an Honoring Dying Man

"Now there stood by the cross of Jesus His mother, and His mother's sister, Mary the wife of Clopas, and Mary Magdalene. When Jesus therefore saw His mother, and the disciple whom He loved standing by, He said to His mother, 'Woman, behold your son!' Then He said to the disciple, 'Behold your mother!' And from that hour that disciple took her to his own home" (John 19:25–27).

When Jesus died, his earthly father Joseph was undoubtedly dead. Although one cannot say with any certainty that Joseph died while Jesus was young, it does seem likely. We know that Joseph was living when Jesus was twelve, for he went with Jesus and Mary to Jerusalem. However, Joseph could easily have died shortly thereafter.

When Joseph died, Jesus conceivably became a carpenter, his father's trade, and provided the family's income. This could very well account for Jesus not beginning his ministry until after he was thirty; he was providing for his family instead of preaching in villages. Since Jesus had provided for his mother in the past, he wanted to be assured she would be provided for after his ascension.

Jesus could have chosen one of his brothers to care for Mary. He had several. But, at this point, his brothers did not believe in him

(John 7:5). Jesus probably chose John to care for his mother so that she would be provided for by a believer. He wanted his mother's caregiver to have the same values he had.

Jesus spoke these words when he was grown. This shows that a person must honor his parents regardless of his age. Obedience by grown children to their parents is not in view here. But, on the other hand, children need to honor their parents: make sure they have what they need to live, make sure they are reasonably happy, and the like.

Jesus teaches us to honor our parents. In the Ten Commandments, God told the Israelites, "Honor your father and mother" (Exodus 20:12; Ephesians 6:2). In speaking of honoring a widow, Paul said her children and grandchildren should serve her (1 Timothy 5:4).

Are you honoring your parents?

Jesus Was a Thirsty Dying Man

Jesus said, "I thirst," so that the Scriptures could be fulfilled (John 19:28). This prophecy came from Psalm 69:21. Jesus wanted to be sure that he fulfilled every messianic prophecy. These prophecies were written so that people could recognize the Messiah when he came. Jesus wanted to be sure we could identify him as the Messiah.

Floggings, such as the one Jesus endured, often produced hypothalamic shock. This occurs when someone loses much blood. It causes great thirst, for the body craves fluid to replace the missing blood. This shows us that Jesus not only fulfilled a messianic prophecy, but that he also suffered a great deal. Jesus endured this suffering on account of our sins.

Imagine being in Jesus' situation. You've not had any sleep, you've been mocked and beaten half-dead, you've had huge spikes driven through your hands and feet, and you are suffocating on the cross. Now, thirst begins. Nothing you can do will alleviate your thirst. There is no way you can get down off the cross and get something to drink.

Imagine being outside on a hot summer day when the sun beats down with all its force. You quickly become thirsty. You will do nearly anything to get a drink of water. But, there's none to be found. No matter where you look, you can find no water. That situation was very close to Jesus' situation; he thirsted, and nothing could reduce his thirst.

Jesus Was a Finished Dying Man

"He said, 'It is finished!' And bowing His head, He gave up His spirit" (John 19:30). Instead of defeat, this is a cry of triumph. Jesus had accomplished all that he came to do. In the Sermon on the Mount, Jesus said, "Do not think that I came to destroy the Law or the Prophets. I did not come to destroy but to fulfill" (Matthew 5:17). Jesus' work was now finished. He had completed his role as Savior. He could now die in triumph.

Everything has been done to provide man's salvation. God needs to do nothing more. All things are ready. Jesus finished his work. The only question is, what are you going to do? Are you going to accept his salvation or reject it?

Thought Questions

55. Why do dying words give a glimpse into a person's soul?

56. Why was Jesus' abandonment by the Father so painful?

57. How does Jesus mediate for sinners?

58. Explain the hope we can have because Jesus forgave the thief with whom he died.

59. How can we have confidence in God when we are in our dying moments?

60. Why did Jesus honor his mother even when he was a grown man?

61. Why was Jesus so thirsty while he was on the cross?

62. What had Jesus finished when he died?

CHAPTER NINE:

Did Jesus Really Rise from the Dead?

Christians believe that Jesus bodily rose from the grave; he was killed on a Friday, but women found his tomb empty early Sunday morning. But, what makes that belief any more valid than any other? Muslims believe Muhammad served as Allah's final prophet. Hindus believe if a person does not get things just right in this life, he has many other lives to try again. New Agers believe an individual can contact the dead for advice on how to live his life.

What makes the Christian's belief any more valid than these other faiths? Is there any more reason to accept Jesus' resurrection than there is to accept Muhammad's office as prophet? Should we believe that women found Jesus' tomb empty more than we might believe in reincarnation? Why believe Jesus appeared to the apostles alive after his death, but not believe that one can communicate with the dead?

But, does it really matter? If Jesus did not rise, don't Christians still have the best lifestyles? Isn't the encouragement that a person receives from his fellow believers valuable, whether or not Jesus lived after his crucifixion? Doesn't the assurance that one's sins have been forgiven give one peace regardless of whether God raised Jesus? Isn't the hope one has in the face of death worthwhile irrespective of Jesus' resurrection?

Far from it. Jesus' resurrection stands pivotal in Christianity. The resurrection established Jesus as the Son of God (Romans 1:4). If he had not been raised, he would not be worthy of worship, his name could not bear our prayers to the Father, and he would not be a good man, because he claimed to be God's Son. He would be nothing more than a liar and a charlatan. If Jesus were not raised, sins have not been forgiven (1 Corinthians 15:17); no one would be able to escape hell. If Jesus is still dead, death has not been conquered (1 Corinthians 15:20–22); once a person dies, he would not have hope of living again. If Jesus did not rise the third day, our approaching deaths should cause alarm and fear; we would not be able to face death with assurance of going to sleep in Jesus.

That hope of the resurrection of the dead serves a meaningful purpose. Beth stood looking at her father's body in the beautifully decorated casket. Memories flooded her mind—she remembered her father taking a day off work to watch her in the school play, working an extra job to send her to college, and giving her away at her wedding. As these memories overwhelmed her, she could think one thing: "Daddy, you won. Daddy, you won." Without Jesus' resurrection, how could Beth view her father's death as victory instead of defeat?

Indeed, Jesus' resurrection gives victory in the face of death (1 Corinthians 15:54–57). But, must one believe Jesus' body was raised? Why not believe that Jesus was spiritually resurrected but that his body was not raised? The Scriptures affirm that Jesus had flesh and blood after the resurrection (Luke 24:39). Jesus had to have a body following his resurrection—the women held him by the feet and worshiped him (Matthew 28:9); he ate with the disciples (Luke 24:43; see also John 21:12–14); Jesus showed the disciples his hands and side (John 20:20); and he permitted Thomas to feel the wounds in his hands and side (John 20:27). The New Testament presents Jesus' resurrection as a bodily event rather than a spiritual one.

But, could anyone other than a theologian conceive of a spiritual "resurrection"? When a Jew spoke of resurrection, he was referring to the body being raised from the dead. The Old Testament provides examples of physical resurrections—Elijah raised the widow of Zarephath's son (1 Kings 17:22), Elisha raised the Shunammite's son (2 Kings 4:35), and when a corpse touched the bones of Elisha, the man stood on his feet (2 Kings 13:21). Where is a spiritual, rather than a physical, resurrection in Jewish Scripture?

In this chapter, we investigate evidence in favor of Jesus' resurrection.

An Identifiable Tomb

First, we must establish Jesus' burial as historically reliable. Most of the crucified were left on the crosses for birds to eat or they were buried in mass graves. Many scholars claim that Jesus' body was either left on the cross to rot or buried with other condemned men. But, if Jesus were not buried in an identifiable tomb, how could the tomb have been found empty? How would anyone know whether or not Jesus was really resurrected if he did not have a tomb? What is the evidence that Jesus was actually buried?

One line of evidence of Jesus' burial comes from an early Christian tradition. The early tradition in 1 Corinthians 15 establishes Jesus' burial as historical. There Paul declares, "I delivered to you first of all that which I also received: that Christ died for our sins according to the Scriptures, and that He was buried, and that He rose again the third day according to the Scriptures, and that He was seen by Cephas, then by the twelve" (vv. 3–4). But, how do we know the early Christians handed this down as a tradition, and does that make any difference? Paul's introduction of the above statement with "I delivered to you first of all that which I also received" (1 Corinthians 15:3) establishes this as an early tradition. "Delivered" and "received" were, in that day, technical rabbinical terms indicating the passing on of holy tradition. Paul's use of these terms shows he transferred holy tradition to these Christians. He alerts his readers that he is giving them a tradition.

This Pauline statement can also be authenticated as an early tradition by its parallel language. The phrase "according to the scriptures" follows both "Christ died for our sins" and "He rose again the third day." Notice also that proofs are offered for both the death and the resurrection—the burial proves his death, and the appearances prove his resurrection. Since many people in antiquity were illiterate, oral traditions used parallel language to allow for easy memorization.

In all probability, this tradition goes back to the earliest days of Christianity, within just a few years of Jesus' death. Paul apparently received this tradition when he encountered the apostles after his conversion (Acts 9:26–28) around AD 32–36. If that is the case, the tradition of Jesus' burial goes back nearly to the time of his burial itself.

But, why does that matter? This being an early Christian tradition is important because liberal scholars want to allow for an evolutionary development of Christian thought. They claim the belief in Jesus' resurrection—and thus his burial—came about slowly and over a long period of time. Legends develop over time, and since, in their thinking, Jesus' resurrection is no more than a legend, much time must be allowed for this legend to develop. However, this tradition shows that the belief in the burial of Jesus came about very early in Christianity.

Jesus' burial by Joseph of Arimathea appears historically reliable. All four Gospels mention this. Why would the apostles have recorded Joseph's burial of Jesus if it were not historically accurate? Joseph was a member of the Sanhedrin, which voted to kill Jesus (however, Joseph apparently was not present when the council voted, for the vote was unanimous). Why would the apostles have cast Joseph in a positive light when the Sanhedrin was angry and bitter toward Jesus? Also, if the apostles had invented Joseph, those who read the Gospels could have easily investigated to discover whether or not Joseph was a historical character.

The Empty Tomb

So Jesus was buried in an identifiable tomb, but how does one know the tomb was found empty? Some claim the sepulcher could not have been empty or the apostles would have taken people there; this empty tomb would have greatly helped people's faith, according to this line of reasoning. But, Peter did contrast Jesus' empty tomb with David's occupied tomb (Acts 2:29–31). And, more importantly, Christianity is a matter of the heart, not of externals. Think about how many externals Christianity involves—baptism takes place in water (Acts 8:36–39) and unleavened bread and fruit of the vine remind one of Jesus' death (1 Corinthians 11:23–27). Those are the only externals in Christianity. Since Christianity does not rely on external "things," why would the apostles have used the tomb to proclaim the resurrected Christ? Also, people have a tendency to revere places. How many school trips have taken students to stand in Independence Hall, where the Founding Fathers signed the Declaration of Independence? How many families have gone to see and to touch (although touching is prohibited by park rangers) the log cabin where Abraham Lincoln came into this world? That tendency would likely have applied to Jesus' tomb—people would have wanted to worship the tomb rather than the Lord who was raised there. Why would the apostles have encouraged that?

However, the apostles saw no reason to argue for the empty tomb. Everyone in Jerusalem knew the tomb was, in fact, empty. Why argue about something everyone accepts? Would you attempt to "prove beyond a reasonable doubt" that George Washington was, in fact, the first president of the United States? No, because everyone accepts that as fact. In the same way, the apostles needed to waste no time arguing for the empty tomb, for the inhabitants of Jerusalem knew the tomb contained no body.

Much evidence supports the empty tomb. The apostles could not have believed Jesus was raised if his tomb had not been empty. Imagine the women coming back to the apostles and saying, "Jesus has been raised from the dead just as he promised." The apostles then go to the tomb and there find Jesus' body lying cold. Would the apostles have left the tomb praising God? Would they have gone back to the women and said, "You're right; he is alive" if they had seen his body in the tomb?

Neither could the apostles have preached Jesus' resurrection in Jerusalem if the tomb had not been empty. Had Jesus' body remained in the tomb, the Jewish leaders, who vehemently opposed the apostles' preaching, could have simply paraded Jesus' body through Jerusalem. If Jesus had been buried in a mass grave, the Jews could have pointed to the very tomb where Jesus' body lay. Had Jesus' body been left on the cross, the inhabitants of Jerusalem would have known about it. How could the belief in Jesus' resurrection have taken hold in Jerusalem if his tomb were not empty?

Consider, too, the first witnesses to the empty tomb. Women found the tomb empty. People in first-century Palestine considered women to be second-class citizens. In fact, women were not permitted to testify in legal cases. If a man killed another man and only women witnessed the event, the murderer could not be convicted. The rabbis also spoke unkindly of women. They said things such as: "Let the words of the Law be burned rather than delivered to women" and "Blessed is he whose children are male, but woe to him whose children are female." When a person lies, he wants to present his best case. If the apostles invented the empty tomb narrative, why have women, rather than men, finding the tomb empty?

The Jews had to explain away the empty tomb; they had to come to terms with it. They explained the tomb's emptiness by saying the apostles stole the body (Matthew 28:15). In his *Dialogue with Trypho,* written in the second century AD, Justin Martyr accused the Jews of having sent "chosen and ordained men" throughout the world to say that the disciples stole Jesus' body (Chapter 108). If Jesus' tomb were occupied, why would the Jews—or any other opponents of Christianity—need a defense of the empty tomb? But, they had to come up with an explanation, for the tomb was, in fact, empty.

Explaining Away the Empty Tomb

So, the women found the tomb empty. But, is that enough to establish Jesus' resurrection? Couldn't something other than a supernatural occurrence explain the empty tomb? Many scholars think so, and through the centuries, many have espoused theories to explain it away. Let's examine some of these theories.

Could the women have gone to the wrong tomb? They suffered much distress when Jesus died, and since Jerusalem contained many tombs, these women simply confused another one for Jesus'. A gardener at the tomb told the women that Jesus was not there. They construed that statement to mean that Jesus had been raised. They ran back to the apostles and told them that Jesus had been raised.

This theory presents numerous problems. The women saw where Jesus had been buried not even seventy-two hours before (Matthew 27:61). Does one quickly forget where a loved one is buried? Many families are in agony when they bury their loved ones, but they do not forget, even with their agony, where the graves are. The man at the tomb did not tell the women only, "He is not here"; he also related, "He is risen" (Matthew 28:5–7). Also, soldiers guarded the tomb (Matthew 27:62–66). Surely the Jews and Romans would have known the location of Jesus' tomb and could have easily corrected any mistake by the women. Could we really expect that the apostles would have begun preaching that Jesus had been raised without first investigating the tomb? And, if the women went to the incorrect tomb, those who wanted to squash Christianity could have simply produced Jesus' body and ended Christianity once and for all.

Others say that Jesus' disciples stole his body. After all, the authorities bribed the soldiers at the tomb to say this (Matthew 28:11–15). But nothing causes this concept to be attractive. The theory centers on guards who were asleep while the disciples stole the body. If the guards slept, how did they know who stole the body? Could not anyone have stolen the body if the soldiers did, in fact, sleep? But, the disciples could not have stolen Jesus' body; they did not have the character to do so. When the guards arrested Jesus, the disciples fled because they feared their own arrest and execution (Matthew 26:56). Why, then, would the apostles have been so brave to creep by guards just a few days afterward? How could the apostles sneak past the guards, move the stone, and remove the body? Would the guards not have heard something to arouse them from sleep? Would the apostles willingly endure imprisonment, torture, and death preaching something that they knew wasn't true? The apostles taught (and witnessed) severe punishment for lying—why would they lie about something so monumental when they taught that lying deserved severe punishment?

Others say that Jesus' enemies stole the body. What purpose would this serve? What would Jesus' enemies have done with his body? If they had stolen it, why did they not produce it when the apostles preached about the resurrection? Simply parading Jesus' body through Jerusalem would have ended Christianity once and for all.

In 1768, the Englishman Peter Annet first propagated the "Swoon Theory." This hypothesis states that Jesus never died on the cross. Those who saw him thought Jesus was dead and thus buried him. While in the tomb, he regained his strength. On the third day, he had recovered from his wounds sufficiently to walk from the tomb; this caused everyone to believe that Jesus had been raised from the dead.

How could anyone advocate such a supposition? To accept this, one needs to believe that Jesus recovered from the tortures of the cross while in a cool tomb, without food or medical attention. How could Jesus have rolled the stone away from the tomb's entrance? How could he have overpowered the guards stationed there? How could one in dire need of medical assistance persuade the disciples to believe he was the resurrected Messiah?

Some believe that the apostles merely hallucinated their experiences with Jesus. Many who have lost loved ones often believe that they see or hear their family members. Could the apostles have simply had an episode such as this?

No evidence supports the proposition. Many of Jesus' post-resurrection appearances occurred to several people at once; such simultaneous hallucinations seem unlikely at best. The disciples claimed to have physical encounters with Jesus (see the discussion above of Jesus' physical appearance)—such language does not lend itself to hallucinations. The disciples viewed Jesus' death as final; they never expected a resurrection. Thinking they saw him resurrected when they did not expect it appears to be no more than wishful thinking from the skeptics.

Not all theories need serious refutation. The Passover Plot, first advocated by Hugh J. Schonfield, clearly falls into this category. This view says that Jesus wanted to fulfill the Old Testament prophecies through a mock crucifixion and resurrection. Jesus collaborated with Joseph of Arimathea and a "young man" to convince the world he was the Messiah. The plot turned deadly when a soldier pierced Jesus' side and killed him. The resurrected Jesus is the young man with whom the real Jesus conspired.

Although this theory really falls on its own merit, a few remarks are in order. Surely, the apostles would have noticed that this young man was not Jesus. How much would they have looked alike? And what about the absence of wounds from the crucifixion? Thomas said he would not believe in the resurrected Christ until he saw such wounds (John 20:24–28). Why would Jesus endure crucifixion, all the while knowing that he could indeed die in the process? And, too, many of Jesus' followers did not believe the Messiah would be killed and resurrected; why do something that would alienate many of the disciples?

The Resurrected Christ

So, women did find Jesus' tomb empty. But does that prove he rose from the dead? Not quite. If you found a loved one's tomb empty, would you believe he had been resurrected? Of course not. You would seek a natural explanation for the body's disappearance. Is there any reason to believe that Jesus was raised from the dead?

The apostles did not expect Jesus' death and resurrection to occur. When Jesus began to tell his disciples that he would die and be resurrected, Peter took Jesus aside and said that he would never allow Jesus to be crucified (Matthew 16:22). The apostles could not conceive of the Messiah being killed. They viewed him as a political figure; he had come, in their estimation, to establish an earthly kingdom in Jerusalem. The Messiah could not die. If the apostles never expected Jesus' resurrection, why would they lie and say it did occur? One does not lie about something happening if it was unexpected.

The story of Jesus' resurrection caused the apostles to look horrible. Their actions surrounding Jesus' death and resurrection cast the apostles in an unsatisfactory light. Peter denied Jesus. The apostles fled for fear. The apostles were slow to believe the women's report. Jesus found the apostles, fearing for their lives, hiding from the Jews (John 20:19). Why would the apostles invent a story that caused them to look so bad?

The apostles died proclaiming the resurrection. Many died horrible deaths claiming to have seen Jesus resurrected. Herod Agrippa killed James, the son of Zebedee, with the sword (Acts

12:1–2). Jews beat and stoned James the Less; his brains were finally dashed out with a fuller's club. Matthias was stoned at Jerusalem and then beheaded. Philip, Andrew, Peter, Thaddeus, and Bartholomew suffered crucifixion. Nero had Paul beheaded. Why would they knowingly die for what they knew to be false? If they had simply kept their mouths shut about the resurrection, they never would have endured such torture. Why would they say that Jesus was raised from the dead if they knew otherwise?

Paul, even though he had persecuted those who believed in the resurrection, became a believer himself. Luke, Paul's traveling companion, recorded that Saul (later known as Paul) "made havoc of the church, entering every house, and dragging off men and women, committing them to prison" (Acts 8:3). Paul himself admitted to having been a "blasphemer, a persecutor, and an insolent man" (1 Timothy 1:13). He despised Christians, their Lord, and all they stood for. Then, he converted to Christianity.

Paul converted to Christianity after Jesus appeared to him (1 Corinthians 15:8). What explanation accounts for Paul's vision of Jesus? Perhaps he just hallucinated—he was fatigued from his trip to Damascus, so maybe he mistakenly thought he saw the resurrected Christ. Why would Paul believe he saw a Lord whom he did not accept? Throughout the centuries, many believers have claimed to see Christ; hallucinations undoubtedly account for nearly all—if not all—of these visions. However, the difference between those visions and Paul's is that Paul did not believe. A person does not just hallucinate what he does not believe.

Perhaps Paul misled the world about Jesus appearing to him. What would he have gained by doing so? He did not gain fame, for he was on his way to gaining fame in Judaism; he had advanced beyond many of his own age (Galatians 1:14). He did not gain wealth, for he did not preach for money (2 Corinthians 12:14). He did not gain an easy lifestyle, for he traveled widely and faced much persecution (2 Corinthians 11:22–33). He did not gain friends, for his friends became his enemies. No logical explanation can be found for Paul's conversion other than an appearance by Jesus.

Jesus has been raised from the dead. He deserves worship. He bears our prayers to the Father. He was a good man. He has forgiven our sins. He has conquered death. We can die in hope, instead of fear, because women found the tomb empty. These women found the tomb empty, for Jesus lives.

Thought Questions

63. Why is the resurrection so pivotal in Christianity?

64. In what ways does Jesus' resurrection give us hope as we face death?

65. How do we know Jesus' body was raised instead of just his spirit?

66. What line of reasoning suggests the empty tomb?

67. What is important about the empty tomb tradition being established early?

68. Why did the apostles not take people to see the empty tomb?

69. Why is the women's testimony valuable?

70. Explain and refute various theories for the empty tomb.

71. Why did the apostles not expect the resurrection?

72. Would you die for something you knew was false?

73. What evidence for the resurrection does Paul's conversion provide?

CHAPTER TEN:

He's Alive

Some time ago, people claimed they saw Elvis everywhere they turned. He pumped gas at the local 7–Eleven. He sat down to coffee and doughnuts at Dunkin' Donuts. He worked out at the YMCA. He bought groceries at Kroger. He watched crowds place flowers on his grave.

Sadly, many people believed these reports. They kept their eyes open so they, too, might get to see the "King." These believers gobbled up tabloids to learn everything they could about these Elvis sightings.

Elvis has been dead since the 1970's. He has not been to the 7–Eleven, Dunkin' Donuts, the YMCA, Kroger, or Graceland. But, Jesus lives. Granted, he died, but he rose back to life. Just as Elvis was spotted alive, so was Jesus. But, unlike Elvis, Jesus actually lived after his death. In this chapter, we explore how the story of Jesus' resurrection is abnormal.

An Empty Tomb

"Now on the first day of the week, very early in the morning, they and certain other women with them, came to the tomb bringing the spices which they had prepared. But they found the stone rolled away from the tomb. Then they went in and did not find the body of the Lord Jesus" (Luke 24:1–3). Some women went to the tomb very early Sunday morning. The text literally says they went to the tomb at "deep dawn," which occurs before sunrise. This shows their earnestness to pay Jesus' body respect; they did not want to wait any longer than necessary. No doubt these women would have gone the day after the crucifixion; however, Jesus died on a Friday. The women were required by the Mosaic Code to rest on the Sabbath (Exodus 20:8–11).

The women came with spices they had prepared. In this time period, spices were used to preserve bodies. The women could not complete their work on Friday, for "the Sabbath drew near" (Luke 23:54). The Sabbath began at sunset on Friday evening. Thus, these women needed to return to their homes and rest on the Sabbath, according to the commandment of Moses. But, now they come to finish preserving the body.

When the women arrived, they found the stone had been rolled away from the tomb's entrance. In Jesus' day, the deceased were often placed in caves. In this method of burial, a large stone was placed at the tomb's entrance to prevent both grave robbing and the escaping of the stench of decaying bodies. These women fully expected to find the stone covering the tomb's entrance. Mark informs his readers that the women worried about how to move this large stone (Mark 16:3). Imagine their predicament: they were the "weaker sex" and would have to move a large stone from Jesus' tomb. But, when they arrived there, the women found the stone had already been rolled away.

Since the stone had been removed, the women entered the tomb, but they failed to find Jesus' body. Therefore, they were greatly perplexed. These women could not conceive what could have occurred. Imagine going to lay flowers on a loved one's grave on Memorial Day. You have spent hours finding just the right arrangement. When you arrive at the burial site, you find that the headstone has been moved, dirt is piled up on one side, and the grave is empty. Imagine your bewilderment. Who has stolen your loved one's body? Who could have done such a thing?

This is what makes this story odd. Loved ones just do not find tombs empty. Once a body has been placed in the earth, it remains there. Likewise, this group of women found this situation odd. Why would Jesus' tomb be empty? What could have happened to his body?

A Living Corpse

"And it happened, as they were greatly perplexed about this, that behold, two men stood by them in shining garments. Then, as they were afraid and bowed their faces to the earth, they said to them, 'Why do you seek the living among the dead? He is not here, but is risen! Remember how He spoke to you when He was still in Galilee, saying, "The Son of Man must be delivered into the hands of sinful men, and be crucified, and the third day rise again"'" (Luke 24:4–7). While the women pondered the empty tomb, two men in shining garments appeared to them. Matthew identifies one of the young men as an angel (Matthew 28:5). Their bewilderment would end; they would understand the tomb's being empty. But, before they comprehended it, the women were afraid and bowed their heads. Put yourself in their shoes. You go to a loved one's grave. You find nothing as you expect it. As you stand in bewilderment, two men in bright vestments appear. You would shake with fright. No wonder these women bowed their heads out of fear.

While these women were afraid, the angels spoke to them and gave them hope. They asked the women, "Why do you seek the living among the dead?" The women had come to embalm Jesus, but Jesus was no longer dead. No one embalms the living. Neither does one seek for the living in a cemetery. The angels say, "Wait a minute. You came to pay respect to the dead. Jesus is not dead. He's alive."

The angels reminded these women of Jesus' prophecies. He promised to be raised. After Peter confessed his faith in Jesus, "Jesus began to show to His disciples that He must go to Jerusalem, and suffer many things from the elders and chief priests and scribes, and be killed, and be raised the third day" (Matthew 16:21). Jesus promised that after he had been raised, he would go before the disciples to Galilee (Matthew 26:32; Mark 14:28). But, the apostles failed to believe Jesus. Just as he promised, he had been raised.

Jesus had told them that he must be crucified and resurrected.

His resurrection fulfilled prophecy (Acts 2:24–31; 1 Corinthians 15:3–4), signified that he was indeed the Son of God (Romans 1:4), and brought salvation from sin (1 Corinthians 15:17). The tomb was empty, for Jesus was alive.

This makes this story odd. Corpses just do not rise from the dead. No one goes to the cemetery, finds angels sitting on the headstone, and hears them say, "He is not here. He is risen." This just does not occur.

Preaching Women

"And they remembered His words. Then they returned from the tomb and told all these things to the eleven and to all the rest. It was Mary Magdalene, Joanna, Mary the mother of James, and the other women with them, who told these things to the apostles" (Luke 24:8–10). The women remembered Jesus' words. They had heard his prophecies. Like the apostles, they probably failed to grasp that Jesus' role as the Messiah meant that he would die and be resurrected. The apostles had great difficulty believing that Jesus would die and be raised before the events occurred. When Jesus told his disciples he would die and be resurrected, the disciples "were exceedingly sorrowful" (Matthew 17:23). Why would they have been sorrowful if they understood what was going to take place? The women, like the apostles, probably had a hard time believing the Messiah would actually die and be raised back to life. But, after the resurrection, they remembered what Jesus had taught. They now knew this was part of God's plan.

Women, of course, cannot stand in pulpits to preach (1 Timothy 2:11–12), but they can do much for the Lord. Priscilla and her husband Aquila explained to Apollos the way of the Lord more perfectly (Acts 18:26). Phoebe served the church in Cenchrea (Romans 16:1). Mary labored much for Paul and his companions (Romans 16:6). The women mentioned here in Luke also did much.

The women went from the tomb and told the eleven and the rest what had transpired. Imagine that your child becomes seriously ill. The doctors examine him before handing down their diagnosis: leukemia. You watch your son's energy fade. He no longer runs and plays. He no longer smiles. He is dying before your eyes. He dies peacefully in his bed, surrounded by you and the rest of his family.

You call the funeral home, and they come to take his body away. You go to the funeral home to make the arrangements for your son's funeral. As you walk into the funeral home, the mortician sets you down and says, "We started to embalm your son, but he started to live again. Your son is alive." The funeral director restores your son to you.

As you leave the funeral home, you tell everyone your good fortune. You stop strangers on the street and tell them what has occurred. You call your family and friends and tell them what has happened. You want everyone to know that your son who was dead is now alive. Likewise, these women could not restrain themselves. They had to tell the apostles what had taken place.

These women were so excited that they just could not keep their mouths shut. We need men and women today who get so excited about Jesus that they cannot keep their mouths shut. God wants Christians to be like these women. When Jeremiah tried not to speak of the Lord, God's word was in him like a burning fire and he could not keep it back (Jeremiah 20:9). David did not restrain his lips (Psalm 40:9–10). Are you telling others about what God has done in your life?

This makes this story odd. Women do not come back from a tomb and say that the one whom they went to honor has been raised. Women do not preach. This story presents itself like no other.

Unbelieving Apostles

"And their words seem to them like idle tales, and they did not believe them. But Peter arose and ran to the tomb; and stooping down, he saw the linen cloths lying by themselves; and he departed, marveling to himself at what had happened" (Luke 24:11–12). The women's words seemed to the apostles as an idle tale. Medical writers used the Greek term for "idle tale" to describe the babbling of a fevered and insane mind. The apostles thought the women had gone mad. The apostles believed that the women had no idea what they were saying. The apostles did not believe.

This makes this story odd. Here are men who will go throughout the known world proclaiming Jesus as resurrected, and they do not believe! Here are men who will write inspired Scripture about the resurrection, and they do not believe! Here are men who are going to lay down their lives preaching the resurrection, and they do not believe! Unbelieving apostles make for an odd story, indeed.

Peter went and looked at the tomb, saw the burial clothes, and went home amazed. May we, too, be amazed at the crucifixion and resurrection. May we be amazed that Jesus would love us enough to die for us. May we be amazed that God has the power to raise the dead. May we have transformed lives that demonstrate our amazement.

Thought Questions

74. Why did the women go to the tomb so early on that Sunday morning?

75. What do you believe went through the women's minds when they did not find Jesus' body?

76. Explain the significance of the angel's words: "Why do you seek the living among the dead?"

77. Why did the women need to be reminded of Jesus' prophecies?

78. Explain the women's excitement as they left the empty tomb.

79. What makes the disciples' unbelief so odd?

CHAPTER ELEVEN:

Jesus Finds Two Disciples

Each Lord's day, Christians remember the Lord's resurrection. During the Lord's Supper, we remember both Jesus' death and his resurrection. As we worship in song, we sing to a living Lord, not a dead one. While we pray, we trust that the living Lord hears our requests and will answer. We give of our means so that the work of preaching the death and resurrection of Jesus can continue. Preachers encourage allegiance to a living lord.

Yet, the first Lord's day does not resemble the Lord's days now. No one assembled in his "Sunday best" for church and then journeyed to Grandma's for dinner. Instead, some women went to Jesus' tomb to anoint his body with oil, but instead of finding the body, they found two angels telling them Jesus had been raised. The women ran back to the disciples, yet their words seemed like an "idle tale" to the disciples.

Also on that day, two disciples (although not part of the Eleven) walked toward Emmaus. They regarded Jesus as the Messiah, and his death the previous week greatly discouraged them. They discussed between them what happened to Jesus' body. As they discussed these troubling events, Jesus appeared to them. When he appeared to these disciples, Jesus found them as:

Puzzled Disciples

"Now behold, two of them were traveling that same day to a village called Emmaus, which was seven miles from Jerusalem. And they talked together of all these things which had happened. So it was, while they conversed and reasoned, that Jesus Himself drew near and went with them. But their eyes were restrained, so that they did not know Him" (Luke 24:13–16). While these two disciples walked toward Emmaus, they discussed the events of the previous week. They talked and reasoned about what had transpired. "Reasoned" carries the connotation of "debate or lively discussion." Perhaps, one of the disciples would say, "Maybe this all means this," and the other would say, "no, these things mean something else." They did not understand what had happened, but they tried to come to terms with it.

While these disciples talked and conversed, Jesus came to them, but they did not recognize him. Apparently, Jesus' appearance was altered some way by the crucifixion and resurrection. Although Jesus had flesh and blood after the resurrection (Luke 24:39), his death and resurrection apparently altered his body. He could walk through closed doors (John 20:19); when the disciples saw him, they did not recognize him (John 21:4). Mary Magdalene did not recognize him immediately after the resurrection; she thought he was a gardener (John 20:15). Likewise, these two disciples did not recognize Jesus.

These opening verses present bewilderment and discouragement. These disciples trusted in Jesus, but now he was dead. They hoped he would restore Israel's glory, but that could not happen now. They believed Jesus was the Messiah, but how could the Messiah be killed? Nothing made sense anymore.

What a blessing to live in this age! We do not view Jesus' death with discouragement and bewilderment. We understand he died for our sins. We understand his resurrection allows us to be raised at the Judgment. How thankful we ought to be!

Proclaiming Disciples

And He said to them, "What kind of conversation is this that you have with one another as you walk and are sad?" Then the one whose name was Cleopas answered and said to Him, "Are You the only stranger in Jerusalem, and have You not known the things which happened there in these days?" And He said to them, "What things?" So they said to Him, "The things concerning Jesus of Nazareth, who was a Prophet mighty in deed and word before God and all the people, and how the chief priests and our rulers delivered Him to be condemned to death, and crucified Him. But we were hoping that it was He who was going to redeem Israel. Indeed, besides all this, today is the third day since these things happened. Yes, and certain women of our company, who arrived at the tomb early, astonished us. When they did not find His body, they came saying that they had also seen a vision of angels who said He was alive. And certain of those who were with us went to the tomb and found it just as the women had said; but Him they did not see." (Luke 24:17–24)

Jesus asked these men, "What are you discussing? Why do you look so sad?" Their countenance betrayed them. Jesus detected their dejection by looking at them. Granted, Jesus knew their hearts; however, from what we know, anyone seeing these men would have noticed their sorrow.

Cleopas answered, "Are you the only visitor in Jerusalem who does not know what things have taken place?" Visitors flocked to Jerusalem during the Passover. All males were to present themselves before the Lord in Jerusalem during the Feast of the Passover (Deuteronomy 16:16). And Cleopas suspected any visitor in Jerusalem knew what had just taken place. Thus, he asked Jesus, "Are you the only person who doesn't know what's happened?"

Jesus asked Cleopas, "What things have happened?"

Cleopas and the other disciple told Jesus about his life. Jesus was a prophet. A prophet spoke on God's behalf. Jesus spoke for God. Jesus himself said, "The word which you hear is not Mine but the Father's who sent Me" (John 14:24). God "has in these last days spoken to us by His Son" (Hebrews 1:2). Moses promised that God would raise up a Prophet like him (Deuteronomy 18:15); Jesus fulfilled that promise.

Jesus was mighty in deed and word. "Deed" implies that Jesus worked great wonders. Indeed, he was mighty: he fed five thousand with five barley loaves and two fish, he gave sight to the blind, he cast out demons from those possessed, he raised Lazarus from the dead. Being mighty in word indicates the great authority with which Jesus spoke. Jesus had authority, for he spoke from God.

Jesus was mighty before God and the people. His being mighty before God indicates his approval before God. His being mighty before the people shows that he had the approval of the people; they regarded him as a prophet (Luke 7:16). Just as in his early life, Jesus grew "in favor with God and man" (Luke 2:52).

Although he found favor in the eyes of God and man, the chief priests and the elders condemned Jesus to death. They strove to get rid of Jesus. What he taught condemned them. His great following threatened their power. The chief priests and the elders did more than condemn Jesus to death—they carried out that condemnation and crucified him.

Although Jesus' popularity threatened the chief priests and the elders, the average Jew had great expectations. Cleopas and his companion hoped that Jesus would redeem Israel. Notice the past tense here—they *had* great expectations, but now Jesus is dead and he cannot redeem Israel.

Although Jesus had died, some women went to the tomb that morning and brought back astonishing news: Jesus' body was not in the tomb. Moreover, angels appeared to these women; the angels declared that Jesus had been raised. Others went to the tomb and found everything just as the women had said, but the body of Jesus they did not see.

These two disciples—Cleopas and his companion—told Jesus the gospel in a nutshell. Although these events had just occurred, they could repeat the details of the gospel. In this age, we know the gospel far better than these two disciples did. Should we not be even more capable of sharing the gospel than they were? "Always be ready to give a defense to everyone who asks you a reason for the hope that is in you" (1 Peter 3:15).

Perceiving Disciples

"Then He said to them, 'O foolish ones, and slow of heart to believe in all that the prophets have spoken! Ought not the Christ to have suffered these things and to enter into His glory?' And beginning at Moses and all the Prophets, He expounded to them in all the Scriptures the things concerning Himself" (Luke 24:25-27). Although these disciples told Jesus the gospel, they still did not believe. They were not so sure Jesus really had been resurrected. The women had reported the resurrection; others, too, had found the tomb empty. But, these disciples still questioned.

Jesus helped them understand. They were foolish and slow of heart. Their foolishness resulted from their unbelief. In Scripture, a "fool" does not believe. "The fool has said in his heart, 'There is no God'" (Psalm 14:1). They were slow to believe what the prophets had written. The prophets wrote about the sufferings of Christ; they wrote about his resurrection and exaltation. Yet, these disciples did not accept the Messiah's suffering and resurrection as necessary.

God intended for Jesus to die and to rise again. Christ was to suffer, enter his glory, and be exalted to the right hand of God. The Messiah would not kick the Romans out of Jerusalem; there would be no earthly kingdom. His work was not political, but spiritual.

The Old Testament foretold Jesus. It nearly reads as his biography. One can know many details of his life from reading the Old Testament. God intended his death, resurrection, and exaltation. God, through his prophets, said that Jesus would die, be raised again, and be exalted. Cleopas and the other disciple should have been in no way surprised that the Messiah died and that the tomb was found empty.

These disciples began to understand what occurred. We need to look in Scripture so that we can understand what Jesus did for us. If we fail to study Scripture, we will know no more about Jesus' life than these disciples did.

These disciples came to believe in the resurrection Christ. When Jesus and these two followers reached Emmaus, Jesus indicated that he was going to go farther, but Cleopas and the other disciple convinced him to stay with them. When they sat down for a meal, Jesus took bread, blessed it, and broke it. The two men's eyes were opened, allowing them to recognize Jesus. He disappeared from their sight (Luke 24:28-32). They finally understood that the

Messiah would die, be resurrected, and exalted. They went and told the apostles all that had just occurred (Luke 24:33–35).

On June 18, 1815, at the Battle of Waterloo, Napoleon and his troops fought the combined British, Dutch, and German forces under Wellington's command. The English used a system of signals in church steeples, something like Morse code, to announce how Wellington and his troops fared. Winchester Cathedral served as one signal station.

One afternoon, Winchester Cathedral flashed the signal: "W-E-L-L-I-N-G-T-O-N—D-E-F-E-A-T-E-D." At that moment, fog covered the church steeple. Villagers around the church quickly spread the news of Wellington's defeat. But, soon the fog lifted, allowing everyone to read the rest of the message: "W-E-L-L-I-N-G-T-O-N—D-E-F-E-A-T-E-D—T-H-E—E-N-E-M-Y!" Quickly, the gloom of defeat turned into joy of victory.

At the beginning, the disciples knew "Jesus defeated." But, they quickly learned, "Jesus defeated the enemy." Because Jesus died for our sins and was resurrected, death has no hold over the Christian. Although we shall die, we shall be resurrected to eternal life. Thus Paul could write,

> "O Death, where is your sting?
> O Hades, where is your victory?"
> The sting of death is sin, and the strength of sin is the law. But thanks be to God, who gives us the victory through our Lord Jesus Christ.
> (1 Corinthians 15:55–57)

Thought Questions

80. How did the Sunday on which Jesus was resurrected differ from Lord's days today?

81. Why were these two disciples so puzzled over Jesus' death and the empty tomb?

82. Why are we blessed to live in this age?

Jesus Finds Two Disciples

83. Why was Cleopas so surprised that Jesus asked what had occurred in Jerusalem?

84. Why did Jesus not immediately reveal himself to these two disciples?

85. How is Jesus a prophet?

86. Why were these disciples slow to believe the report of the women who found the empty tomb?

87. Why should these disciples not have been surprised at Jesus' crucifixion?

CHAPTER TWELVE:

The Confession of a Doubter

Andy came home from church. His mother asked, "Honey, what did you learn in class this morning?"

"We learned about the time Moses and the Israelites crossed the Red Sea. Moses told the engineers to decide the best way to build a bridge. The construction crew came and built the bridge. When they had finished building it, the Israelites crossed the Red Sea on the bridge. About that time, Moses sent in the military; helicopters and bombers destroyed the Egyptian army."

"Honey, surely you don't expect me to believe that's the way it happened."

"Mommy, if I told you the way it happened, you would never believe me."

In this sophisticated world, many refuse to believe what the Scriptures teach. Many deny the virgin birth; everyone knows that reproduction does not include a virgin. Many explain away the miracles of Jesus. For example, some scholars describe the feeding of the five thousand by saying that Jesus convinced the multitude to share their food. Many in the multitude had food, while others did not. The only miracle Jesus performed was convincing those with food to share with those who had forgotten to bring any. Many claim that Jesus was not the Son of God; he was just a good man who taught many good things.

But, we Christians believe Jesus to be God's Son. Each Sunday, as the emblems of the Lord's Supper come by, we Christians remember the death of Jesus. But, the communion service also reminds us of Jesus' resurrection. We worship on Sunday because Jesus rose from the dead on a Sunday. We take the unleavened bread and the fruit of the vine in anticipation of his Second Coming (see 1 Corinthians 11:26) because he was resurrected.

Although we believe in Jesus' resurrection, many disavow the resurrection. Some claim that the apostles merely hallucinated their visions of Jesus—they never actually saw him raised from the dead. Some claim that Jesus did not really die on the cross; according to these, he merely passed out while on the cross, and three days later he walked from the tomb. Some claim that the women went to the wrong tomb; they saw a gardener there and he told them, "Jesus is not here." When the gardener announced that Jesus was not at that tomb, the women thought the gardener meant that Jesus had been resurrected. Others claim that the apostles just made up the story about Jesus' resurrection.

Likewise, Thomas did not accept the resurrection. On the evening Jesus was raised, he appeared to his disciples (John 20:19–23). Thomas, however, was not with the apostles when Jesus appeared to them. We do not know exactly why Thomas was absent that Sunday evening. But, Thomas likely believed Jesus was dead and gone and his messianic hopes were over. This is certainly plausible, for throughout the book of John, we find Thomas as something of a pessimist. When Jesus went into Bethany to raise Lazarus, Thomas said, "Let us also go, that we may die with Him" (John 11:16). Thomas fully expected Jesus to be killed when he went into Bethany. When Jesus told his disciples they knew where he was going, Thomas said, "Lord, we do not know where You are going, and how can we know the way?" (John 14:5). In other words, Thomas said, "Lord, we're going away. We don't know where you're going. We don't know how to get there. Jesus, what are we supposed to do?"

The disciples told Thomas that they had seen the Lord. The

Greek imperfect tense used here indicates that the apostles repeatedly told Thomas that they had seen Jesus. Perhaps, they kept telling him they had seen the Lord, because he simply did not believe. Thomas refused to believe, and he stated that he would not believe until he saw the nail prints in Jesus' hands and the spear wound in his side.

Surely Thomas trusted his fellow disciples. He had spent three years with them. Wouldn't he have known that they would not have misled him? But, the story of Jesus' appearance to the disciples just seemed too far-fetched to be true. Thomas believed only what he could see and verify. He had not seen Jesus alive following the crucifixion, so he refused to believe. Thomas would need to see Jesus for himself.

A week after Jesus met with the ten apostles, he appeared to them when Thomas was present (John 20:24–29). The doors of the place where the disciples gathered were shut. The apostles likely thought they might die as Jesus did, and they hid from the authorities. Suddenly Jesus came and stood in the midst of his disciples. He showed Thomas his hands and his side. Thomas exclaimed, "My Lord and my God!" Thomas' confession came from personal conviction. He referred to Jesus as "my" Lord and "my" God; he wasn't just everyone else's Lord and God. Thomas believed for himself. He was ready to obey for himself. Far too many accept Jesus as Lord for expediency—that's what Mom and Dad believe, that's what my friends believe, that's what I'm supposed to believe. Not Thomas. He looked at the evidence and believed for himself. We, too, need to examine the evidence and believe for ourselves. When we stand at the Judgment, the faith of our parents or friends will not save us. We need personal faith. We need personal obedience.

God expects us to make a confession similar to the one Thomas made. Jesus said, "Whoever confesses me before men, him I will also confess before My Father who is in heaven" (Matthew 10:32). Paul described the necessity of confession to the Romans: "If you confess with your mouth the Lord Jesus and believe in your heart that God has raised Him from the dead, you will be saved" (Romans 10:9). Faith alone, repentance alone, baptism alone will not save. One must believe Jesus to be God's Son. One must acknowledge that faith to others.

In this chapter, we examine Thomas' confession. In particular, we will study how we can make a similar confession today.

Jesus is Lord

Thomas called Jesus his Lord. In doing so, Thomas could have meant any number of things. The term was used in polite conversation, something like our "sir." It also referred to the masters of slaves. It frequently designated a person as having a high position; the emperor, for example, was "Lord." And the term often alluded to God. Because they were afraid of using God's name vainly, the Hebrews were very careful about pronouncing God's name. When they read from the Hebrew Scriptures and came across the term "Yahweh," they would say "Lord," rather than pronounce God's name. The Septuagint, the Greek translation of the Old Testament, translates "Yahweh" as "Lord." Most English translations of the Hebrew Scriptures follow this custom.

Thomas could have intended one of two of these meanings when he used the term "Lord." He could have been referring to Jesus' deity. The Scriptures do teach the divinity of Jesus. However, since he called Jesus "my God," a clear reference to Jesus' deity, Thomas probably didn't mean that.

More than likely, Thomas uses the term "Lord" as one having high authority; he is one who has the right to be obeyed. The Scriptures teach that Jesus is Lord. "Let all the house of Israel know assuredly that God has made this Jesus, whom you crucified, both Lord and Christ" (Acts 2:36). "God is faithful, by whom you were called into the fellowship of His Son, Jesus Christ our Lord" (1 Corinthians 1:9).

When John wrote his gospel, he was living in Ephesus; he lived his later years there. At this time, Ephesus was a center of emperor worship. John and his readers were likely familiar with processions of worshipers going through Ephesus and chanting, "Caesar is Lord! Caesar is God!" In citing the confession of Thomas, John was saying, "No, Caesar is not Lord. Jesus is Lord," and "No, Caesar is not God. Jesus is God."

Jesus is Lord, one of high authority, and one who has the right to be obeyed. Jesus taught the multitudes as one having authority (Matthew 7:29). After Jesus cast forth a demon, the people of Capernaum said, "What is this? What new doctrine is this? For with authority He commands even the unclean spirits, and they obey Him" (Mark 1:27). Jesus told the apostles, "All authority has been given to Me in heaven and on earth" (Matthew 28:18).

In our own lives, we need to recognize that Jesus is one with high authority. "If we live, we live to the Lord" (Romans 14:8). "He who finds his life will lose it, and he who loses his life for My sake will find it" (Matthew 10:39).

We need to show that Jesus is the Lord of our lives every day. If he is, he will be the most important part of our lives. We will spend time studying Scripture so that we will know how to obey him. We will strive to obey what we read in Scripture. We will seek to make every part of our lives subject to the will of Christ.

Can you honestly say that Jesus is Lord of your life? Is he the Lord of your TV Life—do you make sure that you do not watch programs that take you further from Christ instead of bringing you closer to him? Is he the Lord of your body—does he determine how you use your body? Is he the Lord of your home life—does he determine how you treat your wife and children? Is he the Lord of your work life—does he determine how you make your living? Is he the Lord of how you use your money—do you give him the firstfruits of what you earn?

Jesus is God

By calling Jesus God, Thomas announced his belief in the deity of Christ. At this point, the gospel of John has run full circle. The gospel began with an affirmation of Jesus' deity—"the Word was God" (John 1:14). Now, the book ends with Jesus being declared God by one of his disciples.

Indeed, Thomas made the correct affirmation; Jesus is divine. "He is the image of the invisible God" (Colossians 1:15). The Greek term for "image" (,Æ6fv) literally refers to an emperor's face on a coin. The idea inherent in the term is that of an exact likeness or representation. Jesus is the exact likeness of God, for he himself is God. "In Him dwells all the fullness of the Godhead bodily" (Colossians 2:9). The name Immanuel, by which Jesus was to be known, means "God with us" (Matthew 1:23).

The deity of Jesus has several implications. In the first place, this implies that he is our Creator. We read in Genesis that God created all things (Genesis 1:1). If Jesus is divine, he had to play a role in the Creation. Scripture says that indeed he did. "All things were made through Him, and without Him nothing was made that was made" (John 1:3). Jesus was the means by which God created all things; "by Him all things were created" (Colossians 1:16). Man does not exist as a result of a great cosmic accident. He did not come from some prehistoric organic soup. God, through Jesus, created man.

Because Jesus created man, man has value. Every person—regardless of his race or origin—deserves treatment with the utmost dignity; God created that man. We dare not use a racial slur or despise a man because he is not exactly as we are. When we degrade a person, we degrade the very creation of God. How dare we do so?

Also, because Jesus created man, he has the right to be our Lord. He is the Christian's Lord (notice the discussion above of Thomas' affirmation that Jesus was his Lord). Jesus did not become Lord through improper means. He created man. He has a right to be man's Lord. He has a right to expect man's obedience.

Because Jesus is divine, he deserves man's adoration and worship. The psalmist of long ago declared, "Give unto the Lord, O you mighty ones, Give unto the Lord glory and strength. Give unto the Lord the glory due to His name; Worship the Lord in the beauty of holiness" (Psalm 29:1-2). Millennia later, that admonition still rings true—man needs to worship the Lord in the beauty of his holiness. Since Jesus is divine, he deserves that worship. When the disciples saw him after his resurrection, they worshiped him (Matthew 28:17). After Jesus ascended into heaven, the disciples worshiped him (Luke 24:52).

Does Jesus receive from you the worship he so rightly deserves? Do you meet with the saints on the Lord's day? Or do other things vie for your attention—the golf course, the football game, the television, or the Sunday paper? How can man, with all that Christ has done for him, not worship him? What could be more important than giving to Jesus praise and adoration in light of his great love?

Three women met for lunch on a Monday afternoon. The conversation quickly turned to religious matters and how disgusted they were in the lack of worship attendance at their various congregations. The first lady said, "Attendance on Sunday night is only about half of what it is in the morning." "That's nothing," another replied. "Attendance on Sunday evenings is off by about eighty percent where I go." Not wanting to be undone, the third lady, an old maid, said, "Our Sunday night attendance is so poor that when the preacher says, 'Dearly beloved,' I blush!" Granted, many do not worship God as they should. But, may we worship as we should. May we be the ones who blush if we fail to honor Christ as we ought.

Thomas declared that Jesus was his Lord and God. Because of his encounter with Jesus, Thomas would never be the same. Because he saw the resurrected Lord, Thomas spent the rest of his life preaching the gospel. How are you going to spend the rest of your life? According to John Fox, the author of *Fox's Book of Martyrs,* Thomas preached in Parthia and India, where he angered pagan priests. These priests killed him by thrusting him with a spear. Thomas suffered martyrdom because of his confession of faith in Jesus. Will you be as dedicated as Thomas as a result of Jesus' being Lord and God?

Thought Questions

88. Why do some deny the supernatural?

89. Why did Thomas have difficulty believing that Jesus had been raised from the dead?

90. What is the significance of Thomas' personal confession?

91. What does it mean that Jesus is Lord?

92. How will you show that Jesus is Lord in your personal life?

93. How is Jesus the "image of the invisible God"?

94. What does Jesus' deity imply?

CHAPTER THIRTEEN:

If the Dead Stay Dead

A funeral shakes a person to his core. As a man buries his mother, the memories flood his soul, and the tears flow. He realizes that he will never again be able to go "home." He will never walk through the door and smell his mother's chicken and dumplings. He will never again call his mother and tell her what his children did that day that made him laugh so hysterically.

As a woman buries her husband, she experiences loneliness too deep for words. He always took care of the finances; she doesn't know how to balance a checkbook, how many bills she has, or what her income is. He always mowed the lawn; how does she even start a mower? How does she pump gas? He always did that.

The days following a funeral drag on as though they will not end; every day brings new loneliness and fear. But, the Christian mourns with expectation. He remembers well the inspired words— "I do not want you to be ignorant, brethren, concerning those who have fallen asleep, lest you sorrow as others who have no hope. For if we believe that Jesus died and rose again, even so God will bring with Him those who sleep in Jesus" (1 Thessalonians 4:13–14). When Jesus returns, he will raise our loved ones. We shall be reunited with them at Jesus' feet.

But, what if that's just a myth? What if the dead do not rise?

What if the body placed in the ground never lives again? What if we shall not see our loved ones when Jesus comes again? What if the presumption that our loved ones have gone to be with Jesus to await the resurrection is misguided?

Some in the Corinthian church claimed that this was a misguided presumption; they claimed the dead did not rise. Paul wrote to them: "Now if Christ is preached that He has been raised from the dead, how do some among you say that there is no resurrection of the dead?" (1 Corinthians 15:12). These heretics apparently robbed many Corinthians of hope. These Christians had loved ones who died, and they grieved believing that the Resurrection Day was approaching. Then came these false teachers who said, "Wait a minute. The dead never rise. Your loved ones will remain dead." Those who mourned and accepted this view lamented even more deeply.

Some groups in antiquity denied the resurrection. The Greeks believed that the spirit lived after death, but the body would never be resurrected. The Sadducees denied the resurrection of the dead. Some in the Corinthian congregation had bought into these philosophies, and they espoused them to their brethren. Paul takes issue with these heretics. He talks about the mistaken belief that the dead will never rise. He exposes this view as baseless. In doing so, he strengthens the Corinthian Christians. Paul says that if the dead stay dead:

The Christian's Lord is Dead

"But if there is no resurrection of the dead, then Christ is not risen" (1 Corinthians 15:13). If these teachers were correct, then none of the dead—including Jesus—were raised. But, if the dead are raised, then Jesus has been raised. One could not have it both ways. Jesus was either raised or he was not. If he was raised, all the dead will be raised. If he were not raised, then none of the dead will be raised.

If Jesus remains in a Jerusalem grave, he never was the Son of God; the resurrection demonstrated that he is the Son of God (Romans 1:4). The implications of Jesus not being the Son of God boggle the believer's mind. If he were not the Son of God, Jesus was nothing but a farce. He claimed to be God's Son (John 10:36), but if he were not raised from the dead, he falsely made that assertion. If he lied, what type of moral teacher was he? Why obey a single word he taught? He would have no right to speak concerning morality.

If Jesus were not the Son of God, he does not deserve our worship. Each Sunday, millions throughout the world gather to worship Christ. But, if he is still dead, why does he merit worship? He would be no different from Confucius, Buddha, or Muhammad. He might have had good things to say, but if he did not conquer death, why bother honoring him as God?

If Jesus were not raised from the dead, he will not judge us. God has given assurance to the world of judgment through Jesus' resurrection (Acts 17:30). If Jesus is dead, and hence unable to judge the world, we can live how we choose. If Judgment Day will never come, why not throw off the restrictions of biblical morality? (See 1 Corinthians 15:32.)

The Christian's Faith is Baseless

"And if Christ is not risen, then our preaching is empty and your faith is also empty" (1 Corinthians 15:14). If Jesus never rose from his grave, the apostles' teaching was void. Jesus' resurrection served as the cornerstone of their teaching. At Pentecost, Peter encouraged the Jews who heard him to save themselves, but the foundation of his sermon was that Jesus had been raised from the dead (Acts 2:14–36). At Mars Hill, Paul proclaimed the Unknown God to the Athenians, and he concluded the sermon with Jesus' resurrection (Acts 17:31). But, what if Jesus had not been raised? Could the Jews at Pentecost save themselves? Could the Athenians come to know the Unknown God? Christianity either stands or falls on the resurrection. If Jesus had not been raised, the apostles were not who they claimed to be. If Jesus had not been raised, the apostles could not be trusted.

If Jesus is dead, the Christian's faith is empty. The Christian faith has no point if Jesus were not resurrected. Believing something that is false serves no purpose. There is no point in believing the earth is flat, for we know otherwise. There is no point in believing Abraham Lincoln was the first President of the United States, for we know otherwise. In the same light, there is no point in believing in Christianity if Jesus is still dead.

If the Christian's faith is baseless, he has no hope in despair. When facing mortality, Christians rely on their faith for strength. But, if that faith has no basis, what's a Christian to do in his dying moments? Where is he to turn for strength? Where is he to turn for hope?

The Christian Apostles Lied

"Yes, and we are found false witnesses of God, because we have testified of God that He raised up Christ, whom he did not raise up—if in fact the dead do not rise" (1 Corinthians 15:15). If Christ did not rise, Paul and the other apostles lied about God. The apostles traveled throughout the Roman Empire proclaiming Jesus raised from the dead. But, if the dead do not rise, then God did not raise Jesus. The apostles knew firsthand whether or not Jesus rose from his grave. They claimed to have visited the empty tomb. They claimed to have seen the risen Lord. Paul himself said, "Last of all He was seen by me also, as by one born out of due time" (1 Corinthians 15:8). But, if Jesus did not rise, the apostles never saw the empty tomb or the risen Lord.

The Scriptures present lying as a serious offense. God hates lying. "You shall not bear false witness against your neighbor" (Exodus 20:16). Seven things are an abomination to God (Proverbs 6:16–19); two items in that list deal with lying—God hates "a lying tongue" and "a false witness who speaks lies." When Ananias and Sapphira lied to the Holy Spirit, they fell dead in the presence of the apostles (Acts 5). Paul himself wrote, "Do not lie to one another, since you have put off the old man with his deeds" (Colossians 3:9).

The Christian is Still in His Sin

"And if Christ is not risen, your faith is futile; you are still in your sins!" (1 Corinthians 15:17). If Christ remains in his tomb, the Christian's faith is futile—in other words, that belief system is meaningless. If Christ never rose, the Christian believes nothing that will do him any good. If Jesus is still dead, can we believe any part of the New Testament? If Jesus is still dead, can we believe anything we were taught in Sunday school as young children? Of course not.

If Christ is dead, Christians remain in sin, for the faith necessary for salvation (Mark 16:16; Acts 16:31) is futile. Also, Jesus' resurrection plays a vital role in salvation. Christ had to be raised so he could intercede for believers before God's throne (see Hebrews 7:25). If Jesus has not been raised, we have no hope.

Dead Christians Have Perished

"Then also those who have fallen asleep in Christ have perished" (1 Corinthians 15:18). If Christ has not risen, then the dead in Christ have perished. If God could not raise Jesus, how could we expect him to raise anyone else? The simple truth is that he could not. If he could not raise his Son, how could he raise me? If Jesus remains in his grave, every Christian who has died will remain dead for eternity.

I have preached for many funerals, and I always mention the resurrection when the deceased is a Christian. The resurrection gives hope to the grieving—they have hope of being reunited with the departed. When a Christian learns he's facing death, he turns to the resurrection for hope. But, if Jesus did not rise, those hopes will never come to fruition.

If Christ is still dead, then our loved ones who have died abide in hell. They died in their sins if Christ has not been raised (v. 17). Hell would be the only place for them to go. God cannot tolerate sin in his presence (see Hebrews 12:14). Jesus takes that sin away. But, if he remained dead, he did not remove our sins. Even Christians would be condemned to hell.

Christians Deserve Pity

"If in this life only we have hope in Christ, we are of all men the most pitiable" (1 Corinthians 15:19). If Christ is still dead, Christians deserve great pity. We would be a miserable people. The world should just pick us up to take care of us, because we are too miserable to do so ourselves. If we have been duped into believing something as ridiculous as Jesus' resurrection, we would deserve the world's pity.

Paul knew exactly what he meant. "Why do we stand in jeopardy every hour? If, in the manner of men, I have fought with beasts at Ephesus, what advantage is it to me?" (1 Corinthians 15:30, 32). Paul placed his life in jeopardy preaching the gospel. He fought with wild animals at Ephesus. But, if Jesus occupies a Jerusalem tomb, why should he have bothered? We, too, would deserve pity. Many have given up much to serve Christ. Many have striven to give up sins that held them in their grasp. Many have given up lucrative careers. Many have given up close ties with their families. But, if the dead do not rise, there is no purpose in giving up anything. "If the dead do not rise, 'Let us eat and drink, for tomorrow we die!'" (1 Corinthians 15:32). If the resurrection of the dead does not occur, we can forget morality and live life to the fullest extent, because, after all, there is no guarantee of tomorrow.

How frightening! If Jesus still occupies his tomb, we waste our time in serving God. If Jesus never rose, we can forget morality, but we can also forget hope and peace. Not only would biblical morality make no sense, neither would the hope and peace we have in Jesus. If Jesus is still dead, why share our faith? Why worship God?

But, Jesus has been raised from the dead. Our faith is not vain; the apostles' preaching is not vain. Our sins have been forgiven. The dead in Christ shall rise. Christians are not to be pitied. Certain women found the tomb empty one Sunday morning. That Sunday, Jesus appeared to Mary Magdalene and to the apostles. Forty days later, he ascended into heaven and sat down at the right hand of God. Jesus has been raised, and there is hope!

Thought Questions

95. What is, in your view, would be the most frightening had Jesus not been raised?

96. Why, do you believe, some in Corinth denied the resurrection?

97. What would occur if Jesus were not the Son of God?

98. What would you do if your faith were baseless?

99. Could the apostles have been good men and lied about the resurrection?

100. Why would Christians still be in sin if Jesus had not been raised?

101. Explain why Christians would deserve pity if Jesus were still dead.

www.ingramcontent.com/pod-product-compliance
Lightning Source LLC
LaVergne TN
LVHW041532070526
838199LV00046B/1628